MIXED FREIGHT
Checking Life's Baggage

by
S Paul Klein

PublishAmerica
Baltimore

© 2010 by S Paul Klein
All rights reserved. No part of this book may be reproduced, stored in a retrieval system or transmitted in any form or by any means without the prior written permission of the publishers, except by a reviewer who may quote brief passages in a review to be printed in a newspaper, magazine or journal.

First printing

PublishAmerica has allowed this work to remain exactly as the author intended, verbatim, without editorial input.

Hardcover 978-1-4512-4098-6
Softcover 978-1-4512-4097-9
Pocketbook 978-1-4560-0022-6
PUBLISHED BY PUBLISHAMERICA, LLLP
www.publishamerica.com
Baltimore

Printed in the United States of America

What other writers say about S Paul Klein's novel, *Accidents of Time and Place*:

Paul Klein's *Accidents of Time and Place* gives the reader a tense view of individuals caught in Washington conspiracy phobia. Many of us have suppressed recall of this era. Klein brings it back to life with chilling immediacy.

William Crisp

Author, *Goodbye Vienna*

In *Accidents of Time and Place*, Paul Klein paints a profound and insightful picture of a sleepy Washington DC, and an introverted, wounded war hero who takes up his life as an older student after years of war and service to his country. Hector Collin's travel from coal mine to army hero to older student and eventual writer is a poignant and smoothly delivered story, with extremely likable and well developed characters and an appealing and uplifting plot.

Jean C. Keating

National award winning author of *Beguiling Bundle*

Dedication

For Diane, whose perceptive mind and eagle eye keep me focused, and for Lisa, Caterina, Alexandra and Elisabeth who think I know what I'm doing.

Acknowledgment

Some of the essays in this collection first appeared in the Highland (VA) Recorder, and are reprinted here with permission. A few years after those appeared in print, I joined a group of others in what is now known as the Highland Writer's Group. For nearly a decade we have met weekly (weather and schedules permitting) to read each other's work, to help solve writing problems, to encourage and support each other in the hard business of creating original and respectable art. Without it, Tuesdays would be just another day, albeit a Highland County day. Thanks gang, and especially Shirley, who first brought us together.

Table of Contents

Foreword 13
Preface 15

Part I—All Aboard!

Too Much Talk 19
About Folks In The 'Hood 21
A Time For Wizards 24
On Being an Authority 26
Hats Off! 29
The End Of The World (As We Know It) 32
About Rights and Wrong 34
An Old, Old Story 37
Thank You, America 40

Part II—Tickets

Please 42
Giving Credit Where Credit is Due 45
Who Are You? 47
Why We Work 49
The Dirty Option 52
It's About Time 55
About Invention 58
About Monsters 61

Part III—Window Seat

The American Century 67
About Government 69
About The ABC Murders—The death of education

in America 71
A Super Natural Event 75
Beware of Wolves 78
A New Bird 91

Part IV—Fellow Travelers
Message From a Mouse 85
Birds 88
A Management Theory For The Birds 90
Field Work 93
Dancing With Dogs 96
Walk Rabbit, Walk 101
Doe Eyes 103
Dependence, Independence, and Squirrels 106

Part V—Baggage Car
The Man I Used To Be 111
On Understanding Sacrifice 114
Mr. Inbetween 117
Woodworker's Wood 119
Finderman 123
Fear and the Thrill of Meeting the Challenge 125
In a Word, Yes 129
Living Treasure 131
Time Marches On 133
Sleeping In Chairs 136
Have a Piece Fruit 138
If I Knew What I Was Doing 140

Part VI—Observation Car

About Doubt 145
History On Ice 147
Knowing You Have Wings 149
Diversity 151
Preacher 152
About Trust 155
About The Meandering Path of Coincidence 158
Just "Now" 161

Part VII—Mixed Freight

Making a Mark 165
Free Speech 167
A Christmas Story 168
About Bugs 170
Manners 171
Hey, Joe! 173
Granite in Sandstone 174
Written in the Stars 175
Memory 177
Conversation 179
Why the Chicken Crosses the Road 183

Foreword

In 1992, after nearly 40 years in Washington, D.C., I was able to give up working full-time and begin what is often called "retirement." (I define that as "getting tired again, but from different activities.") In my case it has meant continuing to write, which is how I've always earned my living, but what I wanted to write, in a format other than scripts for films, which was what I had been writing for most of those years.

We decided, my wife and I, to remove ourselves not just from the job market, but from the market area, and have, since that time, lived on a mountain farm in the least populated county in Virginia, and possibly still the least populated county east of the Mississippi River. It does have the highest mean elevation of any county east of that line, and so we see the world from half-way up one mountain, looking at another, and must cross as many as four, depending on which way we are headed, to get out of the county. It is a viewpoint that has perhaps shaped my point of view.

These essays, written over the last decade-and-a-half, are not presented chronologically. Instead I have grouped them around common subjects or themes. Where appropriate (or where I can remember), I have added what might help set the scene or identify the time that prompted the essay in the first place.

Let the journey begin!

Preface

Sometimes you begin an essay or a story or a journey, not quite knowing where you will end up. There is a wonderful proverb, attributed to the Chinese, that warns: "If we don't change direction soon, we will end up where we are headed." Knowing where you are headed often seems to be the most difficult part of any journey.

Suppose you have a vague idea of a goal you want to reach. It may be a location in a distant city, or it may be, as in this essay, an end point of a thought. For me, it seems, there is no end in sight. At least not yet. My life has been, and continues to be, a series of unrealized goals. Not that I haven't accomplished something. Far from it. In fact it seems, my life has been full of accomplishment.

When I was young, from my earliest teen years on, I was in the habit from time to time of looking back over a brief period…a day or week or a year, say…and assessing my newly acquired knowledge. Sometimes it was something I had learned in school, but more often it was something I had gained in insight about myself, or about others.

For as long as I can remember, I have been thrilled by the acquisition of some new skill or piece of wisdom or small bundle of knowledge. I got an actual, physical sensation of pleasure when I realized I knew something I had not known before: learning to ride a bike, or use a new word or even express a new thought. As I grew older, I derived the same sort of satisfaction from when I "connected" with a new kindred spirit, or just someone who shared a particular enthusiasm of mine. Occasionally (and I do mean occasionally), it comes in recognition that I have had an entirely original thought, expressed in a film script or other written document. Original thoughts, especially in a world so filled with information and near instantaneous communication, are not the most easily formulated thing. Just giving words to something before you read it or hear it elsewhere is no simple task.

More than one reader has said, after reading one of my essays, "At the beginning I wondered 'where's he going with this?' But when I got to the end, I realized you had taken me exactly where you wanted to go." But then again, isn't life always like that? We start out thinking we are headed on one direction, only to find, as we go, that there are so many interesting by-roads and detours we simply must take.

We do end up where we are going, you know, albeit by a sometimes circuitous route. Life is after all a journey with only one ultimate destination. And regardless of how many changes in direction we make, we all end up where we are headed. But since the last stop is the same for us all, why not make the trip as enjoyable as possible?

As we travel we pick up, without realizing it, a lot of things we have forgotten about, didn't need, or no longer remember why we have them. It's that mixed freight I now bring to the siding for you to examine. Perhaps there will be something you can use on your journey.

Part I—All Aboard!

Too Much Talk

One of the things we're are slowly learning is that one can have (and share) too much information.

My wife spends a lot of time on her computer and is always asking, "Did you see…," and "Did you read…" I spend time on the computer too, but mostly writing. Nobody reads my stuff and she reads everybody's so maybe I should be more "connected."

Anyway, I'm sure companies have good reason for monitoring the e-mail going out from their employees. We are in an age when nothing seems to be proprietary anymore or even private. I read headlines and stories that appall me, about people who "can't comment because they are not authorized to," and who then go ahead and divulge information they shouldn't even know.

I've been a spokesperson (actually a spokesman, but that was in a different age), and I know how tempting it is to tell what you know or think you know, in an effort to build credibility with the media. The trouble is that when you do that, you lose credibility with your own people, which in turn makes it harder to keep your credibility with the media and so on. It all falls into the category of "responsibility in media," it seems to me. I suppose there are examples from history, from as far back as human speech, demonstrating irresponsible communications flowing from those "in the know." Of course there are those "in the no," as in "no comment," and they are at least as communicative as those who are constantly ready to tell all (if not sell all). The fact is that no matter how much or how little a spokesman is willing or able to divulge, there is at once too little and too much being communicated.

Take the most recent oil spill debacle: everyone took to the air to tell what they knew, and if you listened carefully (and looked endlessly) you would have discovered that, at least after six weeks (when this was written), no one knew much of anything. We didn't know how much was being threatened by the lack of care and control exerted by the various players, we didn't know who took which finger off of what button for how long, we didn't even know if it would be possible to put any finger (metaphorically speaking) in any hole to stop the leak. But we did have endless streams of oil and words that left us feeling coated but not warmed, if you will.

And while we're on the subject of coats: I'm about at the end of my tolerance for white collar types with no ties, in their expensive suits, trying to look like they're really working hard. Go home, get dressed and then come back to talk, I want to say to them. I know you can button your collar without getting dirty fingerprints on it. Whom do you think you are kidding, pal?

Just random thoughts that may appear in an essay (but I'm not authorized to talk about that at this time).

About Folks In The 'Hood

In the spring of 1995, on my way to a meeting on the other side of the Blue Ridge, I was delayed for several days in a small town on top of the mountain.

As I write this, the Fourth of July is still to be celebrated this year. For many around the world there is no such day to celebrate, but for us in America, it is a day to contemplate the wondrousness of what free and independent citizens have been able to create. More than that, it is a time to reflect on what we have become as a people.

If one listens to the news on radio, or watches it on television, or reads it on the front page of one of the national newspapers, it is difficult not to get a picture of America as selfish, lazy, crime ridden, basically immoral. I want to warn against taking such a view, and to share with you just one reason why I think that picture of America and Americans is distorted and untrue.

For nearly three days last year, from about noon on June 27 to late afternoon on June 29 I was marooned atop a mountain in Madison County, Virginia. In the space of a very few minutes flood waters destroyed two bridges about two miles apart, and thus began my short adventure.

At the top of the mountain was one of the few visible structures on that two mile stretch of road. It turned out to be a general store and post office, much like the one here in the village where we live. A few cars and several pickups were pulled up by the store. On the long front porch people were watching the rain while others sat in their vehicles waiting for the storm to ease up. At that point I knew only that the bridge ahead was under water and that even with four wheel drive, I would be wise to get off the road until the rain stopped. I did, and the rain didn't. For most of the next 72 hours. When I decided to go on, it was too late. Not only was the bridge over the Rapidan washed away at both ends, but the bridge behind me, over Middle River, was washed away at the near end. My trip, for now, was over.

The Hood General Store has been the center of the settlement of that name since it was founded in the late 1800's. Members of the Hood family still own and operate the business, and one serves as postmaster. There are perhaps 200 people who normally are residents of Hood, but during the three days I was there only about a dozen of them, who lived between the bridges and were at home that day, were around. Of the eight people who could not get home, two lived nearby, three were from villages just across the Rapidan, and the remaining three were "just passing through."

Were we in danger? Not really. There was no power, no telephone, no running water. But there were good people, the store and nearby residential refrigerators and freezers held plenty of food, and nobody had to sleep in the car or on the floor. We were welcomed into homes, shared hamburgers and hot dogs, bacon and eggs, fried chicken and sandwiches prepared in the store or on the porch on a portable gas grill. For about the first 24 hours I was the Hood telephone coop thanks to my cellular phone, so none of the travelers were without a way of letting the folks at home know where they were, and that they were safe. One of the local people lived just across the Rapidan. As he listened to his wife describing the waters lapping at the front and back doors of their home, the phone went dead. For almost 36 hours he had no way of contacting her, nor could the county rescue squad or sheriff's office tell him if she was safe.

For the rest of us the three days were an inconvenience, an interruption, but nothing worse than that. We fell into an easy camaraderie, exchanging views on a lot of subjects, and yes, we talked about the weather: "Rain," "Harder," "I see a dry spot," and "Think the river's gone down?" Yes, we discussed the weather a lot. But do you know what I found to be the most amazing thing in all of this? Not once in those three days did any of us lose our sense of humor, or complain about our plight. In fact laughter was what kept us going. That and a mutual need to feel safe and not abandoned. And something to do. We called it "Camp Hood—A Summer Camp for Adults," and we all helped out. When water needed to be carried from springs to the store, or when food was delivered to the end of the bridge and we needed to walk across the mud to bring it back to our waiting vehicles, we all lent a hand. We also ferried emergency workers from one side of our "island" to the other, and helped those who wanted to walk out get to the end of the road. And of course, we "supervised" the emergency repairs being made to the Middle River bridge.

So what has all that got to do with the news, and with what kind of people we are? I think it tells us that you have to get out into America to find the Americans: we aren't in the newspaper offices and TV newsrooms. We're in small towns and villages about to be washed away; we are in communities facing the aftermath of tornadoes, or even the results of a demented bomber. And when those things happen, like the people of Hood and those of us who had an enforced holiday with them, we respond from our hearts: good hearts, full of concern and understanding, able to see the future as well as the present, and to know that when the chips are down, America is up. God blesses America.

A Time For Wizards

The lesson we learn from the news stories about failed terrorists who try to blow up airplanes or subways or parked cars is that there really are no wizards.

History has thousands of examples of individuals who engendered fear and irrational thinking in vast numbers of people, but who in the end, turned out to be, sadly, only human. Sadly because we must, in the end, claim them as "one of us." Humanoid, bipedal, articulating thumbs—in short simply men and women of no magical power or even great intellect.

One would surmise that the authorities who let these people leave or enter the country where they hope to bring destruction, were trying very hard to resist the effort to "profile" an individual, afraid perhaps that they might sacrifice some unfortunate citizen just to save an aircraft full of others. Well, they miss the whole point of profiling, it seems to me. The men and women who developed the science of profiling were trying to find short cuts to apprehending criminals. Yes, there are places where people with police powers use stereotyping as a form of discrimination and call it profiling, but the fact of the matter is, those people who fit criminal profiles do indeed exist, and do indeed exhibit patterns likely to predict criminal, or at least, antisocial behavior. It seems better to me to use the tools available, rather than leaving it to fellow travelers or passers-by.

Is there an "upside" to all of this? Will passengers and crew now exhibit only the highest level of demeanor and behavior while in public? That is certainly something to be wished for. We have evolved into a world in which rudeness has become a substitute for cleverness, and insensitivity to others a mark of sophistication. Having abandoned air travel more than a decade ago, I can only go by what I have seen when picking up or delivering others at commercial terminals. I realize that my age evokes a profile of a time when ladies wore hats and gloves, and gentlemen wore coats and ties even when they went shopping, but still I find it unseemly that people in airports today look as if they were going to take out the trash. I have heard the stories of crowded seating, airport delays, and extended flying times, and I even recall taking my coat off and sitting in my shirt and tie on overseas or transcontinental flights myself, but it would never have occurred to me to put on shorts, a tee shirt and flip-flops to go beyond my front door, even if I were going to mow the grass.

A century ago, savants proffered a future in which there would be freedom from drudgery and poverty, and perhaps even from fear. Instead we have come to a point where there are many more things we are pressured to desire, a greater number of options to choose from, and oh, so many more things to fear. It is a world descending, rather than the opposite; a world of too many choices, few of which are without negative consequences; a world with a need for magic, if ever there was such a time.

Instead, as with the failed terrorists, we find there are no wizards, only an occasional hairy plotter.

On Being an Authority

For some years I taught a class in public speaking and presentation. The students were all physicians in a postdoctoral fellowship program learning the nuances of scientific research. The end of any research project is a scientific paper, often presented before peers. Part of that process involves reading the paper and answering challenges from the audience. My job was to teach these very bright men and women something many of them hadn't really mastered: being an "authority."

Part of the training session had each student stand in front of the class and deliver a three-to-five minute speech. Subject was not important, but the manner of presentation was. The presentation was videotaped. After each presentation the whole class would join in analyzing the way in which the speaker had presented. The purpose was to help the students feel at ease with a microphone, a slide projector, a pointer and a podium. Any one of these tools of the speaker's trade can become an impediment; the slides come up backwards or upside down, your feet gets tangled in the microphone cord, the pointer wanders all over the screen, and the podium can become a rock to which the speaker is rigidly attached. A central point I would make at the beginning of the two-day session was that just being on a stage, behind a podium, gives a speaker credibility: "The podium," I would say, "is your authority." It was unnecessary, then, to take valuable audience time to establish other credentials. The members of the audience might take great exception to what you had to say, and attempt in the question-and-answer period to destroy your conclusions, but you began from a position of strength. The audience had to challenge you, not the other way around.

The people who host talk radio shows must have been listening to my presentation. They take for granted that the audience will listen to whatever they have to say, regardless of the truth or rightness of what is spoken. For a guest an appearance on a talk show, especially on television, is a golden key, too. Talk about a book, or a cause, or a problem, and people will rush to buy a copy of whatever you have written, or send money to whatever cause you may be espousing. Why? It's almost like an alchemist, turning dross into gold, I suspect, because if you are important enough to come into people's lives through the magic of the airwaves, you must have power, and power translates into authority.

But something is wrong with this power. People with no more knowledge than anyone else, with less education than many, with even lower standards of behavior or morals or ethics can, by pressing a talk button, influence millions of minds in a moment.

What's happened, I believe, is that objectivity and fairness have all but disappeared from public discourse (a term that in itself denotes refined argument and civility). Instead, we have faux-anger, ersatz outrage and occasionally real menace in what should be an exploration of philosophies, a civilized debate, an examination of ideas. Is there a danger in that style? I believe there is. People can be roused to repeat unprovable accusations as fact, to demand undeliverable pledges from their leaders, to commit unspeakable acts. At the very least, whole segments of a nation can be made to demand change without understanding the consequences, and more importantly, without accepting responsibility for their own part in what happens later. As anyone who has ever gotten caught up in a grudge fight knows, you might vent your frustration and fury in a few short moments, but you are equally likely to end up on the ground, painfully beaten, and perhaps permanently damaged.

Is there a message in this? Yes. Beware of "authorities" with no more standing than the floor on which they rest their feet. They are often sitting or standing no higher than you, and see no more clearly the far horizon through their window. It may be a clear glass or a smudged one, but you can't tell that from where you listen.

There was also a tongue-in-cheek piece of advice I used to give my students: when you get a question from the floor that could easily be your undoing, simply look at the audience, point to the other side of the room, and say: "We haven't had any questions from over there." Beware of the speaker who so blithely redirects your attention; one who cannot or will not answer your questions forfeits his authority. If you accept such an authority you might forfeit your freedom.

Hats Off!

I was thinking about hats the other day, as I lay on the chaise in the sun, and it occurred to me that a new age of hats must surely be dawning.

In the first place, as a man who never wore hats, I have suddenly gained a largish collection which, much to my own surprise, I wear. And the selection is broad enough to allow some choices in style, color and utility.

Many years ago, while in high school, I worked as a clothing salesman in what was then known as a haberdashery. We sold suits and shirts and all manner of manly goods, and a rather complete line of hats. The most popular in those years were known as "snap brim" hats, made of felt or, for the summer, straw. The demanding buyer, however, could select from fedora, bowler, and even the latest in styles, the "pork pie." Stetsons, in North Carolina, were not a commonplace, and in the store where I worked, neither were workingman's caps, berets or even baseball caps. Those were either sold in work clothes stores or sporting goods stores.

Today, of course, the baseball cap, seldom emblazoned with the name of a baseball team, but more likely sporting some commercial product or political statement, is the best example of the word "ubiquitous" I know. In gas stations, hardware stores, clothing stores, department stores—almost any place where goods are sold—you may purchase a cap (one size fits all) and support someone else's business, philosophy or sense of humor. They are a far cry from the top hat of Fred Astaire, or the stove pipe of A. Lincoln. And nothing on the market today even comes close to that symbol of American liberty, the tricorn or three cornered hat favored by the founding fathers. So much for tradition where sartorial splendor is concerned.

My own collection comprises a number of the baseball style, promoting a chain saw, a heavy equipment manufacturer, a foreign car company, a contractor, a couple of hardware stores, and even a furnace, not to mention the fire department and a manufacturer of fire and rescue equipment. Most of these hang in the shop, where depending on the weather, I can choose from corduroy, all cotton or cotton with about three-quarters made of mesh, for summer. I do occasionally don one, especially if I am going to be running something that makes a lot of saw dust, or blows leaves and dirt around, or I am going to be hanging about under a vehicle.

My true preference, however, is for a traditional snap brim, especially made of straw for the summer, followed closely by a crushable affair, either of cotton or wool, which serves well when fishing or hiking. For more formal occasions I also have a straw with a creased crown and upturned brim, as well as a heavy duty model in felt for colder days.

While hat-wearing is a relatively new idiosyncracy of mine, I think it is a "good thing" to do, especially in the summer, my natural head covering not being what it used to be. I don't generally worry about sun burn, being of a complexion that recalls my gypsy ancestors, but it seems appropriate to seek some protection for what is now bare skin where once the dark locks grew. I do have some problems, however.

First of all, the brim (or bill, presumably as in "duck") blocks my vision. Being tall, and perhaps a bit too introspective, I tend to look down when I walk. Tree limbs and low doors have left several permanent scars on my more visible pate, and there seems to be no long-term cure for this particular malady. I do remember to duck for a while after an encounter, but soon that wears thin (about like the hair) and I bonk it again.

The hats with the full brim offer the greatest problems, however. In today's cars, for instance, with high seat backs and head rests, the brim at the back of the hat is in constant touch with the seat, forcing one to either drive with bowed head, eyes cast upward, or to push the hat down low over one's forehead, resulting in greatly diminished vision. The prayerful pose may be appropriate given today's traffic, but it is limiting, and neither position is comfortable.

The other serious drawback is that one has a hard time napping. Every time your head rolls back to find a really comfortable position, the brim stabs you across the back of the head, guaranteeing a quick snap forward, and wakefulness. It might be the true meaning of "snap brim," but more likely (given the wholesale wearing of such, both in and out of doors) it is the real reason for the popularity of the baseball cap.

Now, if there is to be a new age in head gear, I'd like to suggest a high tech version. First, the cover should be of a material one is able to see through. That might help my own problem with bumping into things. Second, the hats should have built-in sensors to determine when it has been brought indoors. Ideally, after making some sort of warning noise, giving the wearer a few seconds to remove it from his head, the hat could say something like: "Please remove your hat." Quietly at first, of course, but eventually loud enough to call attention to the wearer, should he not heed.

Imagine a theater, restaurant, even people's homes in which men didn't wear hats. Now that's something to take your hat off to!

The End Of The World (As We Know It)

Y2K, the non-event of the century, elicited a lot of different plans and programs. The one this essay reviews appeared in a news article in a daily paper in the Fall of 1999.

I read in the paper the other day that a well-known televangelist has taken a very different view of the Y2K problem. He sees that problem as the trigger for a chaotic and world-ending scenario. To that end (if you will allow the pun) he recently announced that in preparation for Christ's return to earth with the beginning of the millennium, he is stocking up on food and ammunition.

Now my relationship with the man's family goes deep, some 300 feet or so, by virtue of the fact that years ago one of his uncles drilled a well on some property I owned north the Reverend's home town. Beyond that, I really don't know the man, so I can't really ask him face to face the questions that the news article immediately raised in my mind.

First, I want to know why he is stocking up. Does he plan to stay around? Especially in what could only be described as a hostile atmosphere, against a set of unlikely odds. So why does this man, one who has preached the second coming, and the promise that Christ will come to carry all worthy souls to heaven, feel that he has to be prepared to stay?

My next question is about how long he is planning to remain behind. Does he truly feel the world will be total chaos, full of fire and brimstone; that the sort of world he has preached about will come? How long does he think he can hold out? Does he envision that terrible period passing and leaving a new, fertile earth? If the end is thermonuclear, either man-made or natural, how long is the half-life?

And the final questions, I guess, concern the ammo. When the end of the world comes, does that mean the Ten Commandments are no longer in play? Who is he planning to shoot? What provocation can this man of God cite that will excuse his discarding the commandment to not kill? Or does that apply, like so many of the other utterances of a man like this, only to those whom he regards as worthy? Armageddon is a well, you know: a deep hole where embattled Jews once protected themselves against invading Romans, and where even Napoleon fought a major battle. Is there something that gives this man the moral position to kill, to be the last man alive? Just what does this tell us about his own beliefs?

Well, it tells me that the $28 he charges for the videotape in which he outlines his plan for the end of the world is something he probably wants in cash, no checks or charges, please.

About Rights and Wrong

In the news recently there appeared one of those wonderful stories I just can't help commenting on. It told of a young boy in California (notice I resisted any pejorative such as "where else?") who had conducted an experiment for a science fair project, in which he exposed fruit flies to an x-ray in order to determine the effects of radiation on reproduction. In the course of his research 12 of the subjects had to be "euthanized" (not just whap, whap) because they had become infected with a virus. Such an occurrence, you see, could compromise the results.

Now lest you think this piece has to do with diseases such as fly flu (a-choo!), or a call for more research into the beneficial effects of chicken soup, let me warn you that the issues here transcend mere scourges like the common cold. What we have here is one of the great moral dilemmas of our time.

As most of us in Highland can attest, flies (fruit or otherwise) are not so easily gotten rid of. In fact they have, in my own mind, become a regular season (the four being Snow, Mud, Dust and Fly, often occurring simultaneously). So if a fly dies, it is often a choice we make without guilt.

The Chinese, you may recall, took a really hard line position during one of their many great leaps forward, and added flies to one of their interminable lists of "olds" to be eliminated. Arming everyone in Shanghai, the target city, with fly swatters, the campaign was one of the true successes of Chairman Mao's leadership. Here at our house we have instituted a similar program, often arming guests with gaily decorated, but lethal, swatters, and urging them to respond to the war cry "fly alert!" Our own great leap forward is annual.

Now, I realize that fruit (*Drosophila melanogaster*) flies and house (*Diptera muscidae*) flies are not the same, and that the fruit version have a long and honorable tradition of aiding mankind's study of genetics. Still, they are no more welcome in a house than their larger relatives. I don't want them eating my fruit, anymore than I want the others eating my house.

Meanwhile, back in California, our young scientist is coming face to face with the realities of laboratory research. After taking the study subjects to his father's lab, and having them exposed to an x-ray, he began the tedious process of watching, examining and recording the findings. It was only after he had completed his research and submitted his results, that disaster struck. No, not the virus which eventually claimed the lives of 12 subjects; much more than that. The *Nuked 12* were no doubt "put down" in a painless and peaceful way B this was California, after all. No, it was the entrance of the Fly Police.

After agreeing that this young man's work represented real science, and that the methods, materials and conclusions were of the highest order—after all of this he was denied the top prize because of (can you picture this?) cruelty to animals. (Anywhere but California this probably would have rated a A!".)

Euthanizing 12 fruit flies that had become seriously compromised with a virus, constituted (according to the review panel) blatant abuse and cruelty, and must not be tolerated. Well! I guess that young man will think twice before he hurts another fly. He might even think twice about pursuing science as a career. Not, mind you, because he doesn't want to hurt a fly, but because he does not relish the prospect of animal rightniks camping out on his lawn, harassing him for applying harsh scientific discipline to his research by removing potential contaminants from a scientific study.

It all reminds me of a time when I had to defend the organization for which I was spokesman against similar (unfounded) charges made by a well-known animal rights group. Two things come to mind. The first is the position of one of the organization's leaders that her own use of insulin, developed at the cost of many laboratory animals, was acceptable because it had been done before she was "aware."

The second was a motto I proposed for the next generation of such foolishness: "Eat Air and Go Naked. Plants Have Rights, Too!"

An Old, Old Story

Every Congress seems to want to eliminate, or at least mess with, programs that benefit the average citizen. Often presidents add it their agendas. This was written during the G. W. Bush presidency, but it applies today as well.

I don't know what it is like today, but in the 1950's, when I lived in Pennsylvania's anthracite country, the county was also a center for some big-time gambling, including horses, poker and "numbers." Reportedly the "mob" controlled the town, and there were several things I heard, but never witnessed, that convinced me there was some truth to the stories.

One was a "tip" a co-worker passed on to me one day, purporting to be the number that would win the pot that afternoon. Now, "numbers," as I understood it, involved betting half-a-dollar that a number you picked would be the winning order at some race track that day. If I understood it correctly, that also meant that if one could be "tipped" to the winner, then the honesty of the race must also be in question. For a lot of reasons, mostly a disinclination to be beholden to some mobster, or to waste even fifty cents on games of chance, I failed to play that number, which in fact, did turn out to be the winner.

Another story I remember involved an elderly woman who lived down the hall from me in the hotel. I would often see her shuffling about, going to the bathroom at the end of the hall, working her way down the stairs to the lobby, and occasionally out on the street, going to one of the nearby restaurants. None of us had "housekeeping" rooms, but there was a housekeeper who cleaned and made the beds. Her name was Mary.

One day, near the end of the month, I was in my room when I overheard Mrs. R, as she shuffled down the hall toward the stairs, talking to Mary. "I don't know what I'm going to do, Mary," she said. "I haven't heard from my son in a week, and he hasn't sent me even a postcard." Mary, who tried not to get too involved in the resident's lives (unless she could hear a really juicy story), responded along the lines of "Well, I'm sure he's ok, missus. You'll hear from him soon, I'm sure."

"Yes, but that isn't what I'm worried about, Mary. It's still three days 'til my next Social Security gets here." The voice now began grinding tightly. "And I only have a dollar left until then. How'm I gonna eat?"

This was in the 1950's and food, even in a restaurant, was very cheap. A dollar would serve for at least a single meal. But that wasn't the whole story. "Missus," as it turned out, was counting on half of that dollar to play her daily number; she wasn't about to waste two days play on something like food. Let the "Social Security" and her children take care of the food. She was going to take care of her "number."

Let's shift forward a year or so. I left the work I was doing in that town and returned to Washington, where I took a position with a national business association. One major thrust of the organization at that time was to abolish Social Security completely, and allow wage earners to "put their money in the market." Now fast-forward nearly 50 years. The theory was somewhat like that being advanced today to divert "a small percentage" of a worker's earnings from social security to the stock market through individual investment. Underlying all of that, it appears to me, is the unspoken objective of eliminating the whole system, and throwing responsibility back to the individual to prepare for the future.

So the question is this: How will privatizing social security benefit people like "missus" back there in Pennsylvania (or anywhere else) who see gambling, on numbers or stocks and bonds, as their answer to the problem? Who will teach them to conserve their money when they are 20, so they will have it when they are 70? The companies that conveniently merge and downsize when their pension obligations get too large? The "entrepreneurs" who sell stocks that have no value?

Or should we, like "missus," just play the numbers? It might, after all, be a better deal. Again, tell me about how good it is to get government out of our pockets. Is it just to make room for Wall Street?

Thank You, America

July 2003. On the road again for the first time since 9/11. We need a tube of toothpaste, a bottle of mouthwash, and something for dry skin. There's the Wal-Mart. Take the off ramp, pull in, park, walk, go down the familiar isles precisely where the products we need are located, walk back to the cashier, pay, walk to the car, drive back to the highway. Thank you, America.

Another day, and the summer heat beats down on the car. We need some sun shades to block the heat from the side windows while we drive, and one for the windshield when we park. There's the Wal-Mart, just up the block. Pull in, park, walk, go right to the automotive section, find the right isle, decide which models we want, go to the front, pay, walk to the car, drive away. Thank you, America.

Still a hot day, very dry. The McDonald's is on the next corner, or there is a Burger King across the street. Pull in, tell the disembodied voice what we want, drive around, pay, get the drink, drive on. Thank you, America.

The Wal-Marts, the McDonald's and Burger Kings and Subways are not local, though as far as the fare is concerned, they might as well be. One is in Colorado, another in Wyoming, others in any state you can name. It saves time (and money), and leaves you more of both to explore local shops, restaurants and customs.

We've been traveling around our native land for the past two and a half weeks, going west beyond the Mississippi and Missouri rivers, much as many earlier citizens have done, on a voyage of exploration and discovery. We haven't discovered new lands, or waters, but we have discovered America.

In the east, much of the middle and western parts of our nation are the things of story and song, of legend and of myth. When you travel about, in search of nothing in particular, you find a great many surprises, especially of a geographical or topological kind.

In Illinois and Kansas, for instance, we discovered what rich farms really look like: vast and green, and served by machines so huge that the average eastern farmer wouldn't be able to turn them around, especially on the farms we are familiar with in our mountains. But even in the Shenandoah Valley, just a mountain away, where fields roll away into the distance, the distance isn't all that far. In the middle west, it seems vast. And that is just the beginning.

As we rolled west, beyond Kansas, we began to experience a nearly terminal case of the "Oohs and "ahs," that chronic disease engendered by unlimited new and exciting images all around.

We paddled our own rubber boats on the Colorado, rode horses (mine was a wild mustang) across the high desert, and looked at mesas and mountains and rocks and rivers from the car, from afoot and from the saddle. What we saw were ancient dwellings of the Anasazi, canyons and cliffs and incredible shapes of rock that cause the heart to swell and the mind to sing; places that we had heard about, read about but could not really imagine. Just the names are sufficient: Grand Tetons, Yellowstone, Black Hills and Badlands. There were high deserts and the great plains, the Mississippi and Missouri, the Snake and the Sioux rivers, Crow and Cheyenne and Lakota and other tribal names, along with Little Big Horn and even small George Armstrong Custer and the 7th Cavalry. Seeing all of that, riding through some of it on horseback, gliding down a famed river (though not its most impressive part), much of it from the wonderfully revealing roads our car traveled so easily, all of that helps to recapture at least the sense of what America is.

But this is a big land. It takes eyes that can see far; eyes that envisioned a new civilization, not just a field of grain (or gain). We imagined ourselves on the seat of a wagon, pulled by two or four oxen, seeing a distant mountain loom never closer, at six miles a day. Perhaps if we had been moving like that we wouldn't have been nearly so impressed; our senses might have adjusted to the slowly growing Rocky Mountains that took weeks, not hours to reach. But I don't think so. I believe that even the most road-weary immigrant was awed by the snow-topped peaks, the near vertical heights, the red and yellow and parching white of striated, flat-topped mesas and apparently bottomless gorges and canyons. How could one not be? Still they persevered.

Imagine coming to what are called the "Badlands." Miles of sharp, bleached canyons and mesas, places where you can look down and see only a maze of dry, twisting, narrow paths. How to get through, how to find one's way back, how to survive to the other side? Is there "the other side?" These were men and women of oak and iron, these pioneers who came to this land of rock and sagebrush and cotton wood. Yet they crossed and recrossed these plains and deserts. They even staked claims and built huts that became homes, and trails that became roads, and they built lives. American lives. Their origins were in every country, their expectations exceeding any a people had ever known. They gave to the land, but the land gave back many times over. Between the people and the land there arose a nation. It could not have happened without both.

Thank you, America.

Part II—Tickets Please

Giving Credit Where Credit is Due

This originally appeared in print about 1997. I don't think it takes a degree in either economics or business to see the danger in imprudent lending. The danger, however, is as always, to ourselves.

Recently I chanced upon an article in a daily newspaper about a dog that was offered a credit card by General Electric. The dog, with the improbable name of Janosch Von Braunen III, lives at a kennel in Monroe, N.C., where he presumably authorizes the purchase of feeding dishes, doggie treats and such items of fashion as collars, leads and booties.

What makes this story relevant to our times, as they say, is that it underscores something I have long thought was at the bottom of our economic troubles: easy credit for people who have even easier consciences. For years I have received unsolicited offers of credit cards. Not that they aren't useful, and not that I don't have one, but the one I use was chosen by me, based on the bottom line, not the color of the card. In the beginning, when I first started getting these "too good to be true" offers (they usually were), I would return them with a letter to the president or CEO with the admonition that they were dooming this country to economic disaster by putting such tools in the hands of irresponsible and uncreditworthy individuals. I never received a response, you understand, but I would feel better about making my feelings known until I would receive another card offer from the same company. Evidently they were reaffirming their faith in my good name.

Now mind you, this was in the 60s. I began my working life in the 40s, when credit was still something our depression-era parents had come to view with very mixed emotions: it was at once a savior in times of great need, and a rock around your neck every minute you used it. When I wanted to open a savings account in my hometown, I was told the bank would review my application and let me know. And this was a bank where my father had banked since about 1918. I went through the same drill later, when I applied to open a checking account, but by then I had established my credit by saving money, and the bank took a much less squinty-eyed view of my request. But they reviewed it, even so.

Today our economy is a very fragile thing indeed. A dip in sales, a rise in unemployment, no matter how small, can send businesses into downward spirals. No one seems to have any savings to speak of, and everyone has unpaid debts sitting like vultures over their shoulders. And now even a dog can get credit. I will say this for GE, though. Janosch is 14, mature in dog years, so perhaps the credit investigators decided he was fiscally responsible, which is more than I can say for the companies that court college freshmen with the same offers.

One final thought: why does a company that makes toasters want to give away credit cards? Do they think they can butter their bread on both sides?

Who Are You?

This was written during an earlier economic downturn, but I believe the proposed system of analysis is still valid.

I happened on a friend the other day, who was doing some chores around his maple syrup manufacturing plant. He was dressed for the job in the usual kind of scruffy clothes one keeps for getting dirty, and I noted that on his shirt front were badges identifying him as a technician named "Bob" for a company I had never heard of. Since Bob is not his name, I made a small joke about not knowing who he was. He explained that an industrial laundry in a nearby town sold these shirts, and other work clothing, at ridiculous prices; three shirts for $2.25.

A little investigation at the laundry revealed several things: a store, in addition to the laundry in-take desk, racks of work shirts, pants, even coats and ties, all cleaned, all in good condition, almost all identified with pressed-on badges for some company and some worker. The shirts are sold three to a bundle, matched by color or material, neatly tied with string.

Sorting through the stacks of shirts one can come up with matching shirts from three different companies, and three different workers. Then there are the sets in which all three shirts are from the same company, with the same worker's name. There is significance here. Obviously Dave or Chris or Sam no longer work for Johnson's Lumber, or Diley's Garage or any of the other folks whose shirts are now for sale.

What this suggests is that here is a new way of measuring the economy; one far more accurate than Mr. Greenspan uses perhaps. From a random sampling of shirts no longer needed, one can deduce which industries are shedding people, who is no longer employed by name, in fact a very personal sort of unemployment statistical set. In addition, I suppose, one can get some idea of how the rest of the economy is doing, and what types of industries are downsizing, simply by looking, over a significant period, to see how the company badges change. Does one name keep coming up in the stacks of green shirts? Is it a color change or an industry downchange? Are the shirts most available from the dirty fingernail set, or are they from something like electronics service and repair or delivery services? Are goods and services declining as represented by a plethora of badges representing those markets, or does it perhaps signify some marketplace response to a company's individual performance? All of these, of course, are questions best answered by people known as "pundits." I'm just a writer. Today I'm working for Instant Telecommunications. My name is Ron.

Why We Work

    During World War II the army produced a film series called "Why We Fight." I recently read an interview with a skier who thought that any interference with his skiing, in the interest of safety and good sportsmanship, would (in that succinct way young people have with words) "...totally annoy me..." "You only live once," he is reported as saying. "It's an adrenaline-based sport. That's how I get my kicks." So the question that schusses into my mind is, "why do we work?"

    A long time ago I was involved in auto racing at what the Brits call a "club level." That means we were all amateurs, most of us drove the cars we raced on Sunday to work on Monday, and our tracks were either shopping center parking lots (this was in the days when stores were closed on Sunday), or were held over public roads (with police permission). These events were organized by sports car clubs ostensibly for the fun of competing with others in similar vehicles, against a clock. There were also closed-track events, road courses often laid out with hay bales on air strips or over purpose-built courses included in more conventional oval tracks. Even these races were for glory, not dollars. The value of the trophies awarded was nowhere near the cost of running your car, even if the event lasted only 2 to 3 minutes.

    Under the rules, any stage of any event, from start to finish, could be questioned by a formal protest filed at the time by a competitor. One night, after running a event called a Rallye, my navigator and I were presented with trophies for one of the three top places in the event. It meant that we had covered each stage in almost perfect time and average speed for each leg of the event. After the awards had been given out, and we were all sitting around eating, drinking a beer and telling war stories, a representative of the organizing club found me and said that a protest had been lodged by one of the losers, and on the basis of the protest, my partner and I had been bumped from second place to a position below third place. He was really sorry, and he apologized, and he was very worried about having to take back the trophies and so on. He seemed most distressed, until I said, "Oh, ok. Fine with me. I wouldn't want something I didn't win honestly," and other expressions of good will and sportsmanship. My partner and I were disappointed, sure, but no more than we had been surprised to finish in the top three to begin with. Anyway, the sequence of events got me thinking about work and workers. The young man in the ski story reawakened those thoughts, and the conclusions I had drawn from them at the time—conclusions I still hold valid today.

At the time I was working for a small private company, but I had come to it after progressing through other jobs, including one for a national business organization. While with the larger employer I found that many of the people who worked there were members of things like bowling teams sponsored by the company. I even went a few times as a substitute, but couldn't really get excited by either the game or the seriousness with which others took it. The same for company-sponsored softball and other games. Basically I was on the job to work, I liked my work, I enjoyed the rewards it brought, and when I wasn't working (which wasn't often) I really wanted to be away from the people I worked with all the time, under no pressure to succeed or excel, but just to have fun. That was what the racing was all about, for me.

So I evolved what I later came to think of as the bowling-shirt theory of employment: people can be attracted to a company because they like bowling shirts the company buys. In other words, people who don't find themselves in creative, challenging positions would look for companies that offered benefits such as recreational opportunities. These activities have the effect of disarming employee angst, and helping to bind the employee to the job. Eventually the play-time becomes the reason for the pay-time.

Relating that to the 90's isn't so difficult. You just need to remove the company from the equation. Since so many companies have demonstrated their lack of loyalty to their employees in the last decade, that shouldn't be hard. Then apply the current yardstick of satisfaction, "what's in it for me?" and you have the current version of the bowling shirt theory. Is that a good enough reason to work?

I said to the club official, that night so long ago, that I really wasn't upset (he was very afraid I was). "I don't know what the rest of these people do," I said, "but I don't take these trophies home and melt them down and put them in the bank on Monday. That's not how I earn my living. That's why I work."

The Dirty Option

A friend who lives in a major urban area visited us recently, driving a newly acquired econo-wagon. In the process of looking for the right car, she told us, she had seen a demonstration of an imported "sport utility vehicle" (known as UTE, in the trade) At around $60,000 it was well beyond her means, but she was fascinated by the dealer demonstration area which included a man-made hilltop. If you were interested the salesman would let you drive up and over the top, to demonstrate the vehicle's mountain goat qualities. Knowing of my interest in all kinds of people movers, she thoughtfully brought along the highly styled sales brochure, and we all looked at the exotic things you could have as either standard or optional equipment for your trip to the grocery store via Mt. Kilimanjaro and I-81 (either one may be a test of your driving skill).

In addition to the more usual exotica, such as leather seats and fine carpets, this particular vehicle has a suspension system you can adjust for load and ground clearance, outside mirrors that automatically reposition themselves to show you the curbside when you shift into reverse, and a whole box full of "comfort" items you probably never thought you would need (and probably don't).

I'm sure you have seen the ads for an American made "UTE" demonstrating the vehicle's ability to drive straight across rocky fields, piles of boulders, even swamps. But who buys these "trars" (my own word: being neither truck nor car, and a "UTE" being either an Indian tribe or a young person who lives in Brooklyn)? Since most Americans live in cities or distinctly urban areas, these vehicles, like pickup trucks, are used primarily as go-to-work/go-to-the-store sorts of vehicles. I guess it is a matter of image, more than anything else: how we like to be seen.

I can't deny that we bought one of these trars (American made) when we were preparing to move here full-time, but that was primarily because our only other car was a two-seater, and the idea of something as roomy as a sedan with the 4-wheel drive and load capacity of a small truck seemed right for Highland County. It has proven to be a mixed sort of "right," with neither the comfort of a car nor the convenience of a truck, but it serves. It does get up and down the driveway when the snow is deep enough to need plowing, and we can take visitors over roads like 620 from Doe Hill to 614 and not worry about getting through, and it makes an impressive showing between here and the firehouse, so it wasn't a totally irrelevant purchase. And it has most of the other options available at the time except leather seats and an automatic transmission: electric windows and door locks, anti-lock brakes, and so on. And I personally enjoy a driver's seat I can get into without performing some combination of the Limbo and the Twist. These vehicles definitely have their place here in the country.

There is one option, though, that I think all the manufacturers have missed out on. If you look at the ads in print or on tv, these vehicles are always trekking across some dusty, dirty, muddy track through the wilderness (much like the road we live on), throwing up clouds of dust or muddy spray. The view through the windshield is obscured, except for the sparkling clean arc of the wiper blades (where do they get those wiper blades? I've never been able to buy any except the ones with built-in gaps and streak-makers). One thing about driving around here—the topsoil always comes back home! I wash the cars whenever I can, and pounds of dirt and little stones sluice off onto the gravel, keeping at least some of the runoff in check. But not everyone lives in the country, so for those city dwellers who might feel guilty about driving a truck-equivalent in commuter traffic, here is a proposal for any manufacturer bold enough to try it: why not make a kind of stick-on set of panels that are sort of brownish-tan, knobbly plastic? And some semi-transparent ones for the windshield and windows? Not only would you not have to wash your vehicle, it would give you the feeling that you had at least been someplace to justify the purchase.

It would be called "The Dirty Option."

It's About Time

This started out to be about what happens when you get a car repaired. Then I sort of moved on to a somewhat larger issue, and if we get to the car repair story it will only be a sidelight on what I perceive as an otherwise more universal problem.

50 years or so ago, most American manufacturing was still accomplished as nearly as possible "in-house." That is to say, a company began with an idea and ended with a product, most or all of which was done by departments or branches under the corporate umbrella. Henry Ford, that inventor of so much of modern industry, was perhaps the greatest proponent of this idea. The huge River Rouge plant was fed by energy generated by Ford-owned coal, used Ford-manufactured steel and Ford-grown rubber, and produced vehicles using Ford-made parts. Of course all of this began in a era of company stores and company housing, a privately owned welfare program of sorts. Students of such things can also cite the other aspects of this "benevolent" industrialization, and historians will point to the system employed best perhaps by the Medici family in renaissance Italy as the historical precedent, but for our purposes the American example will do.

Now back to the present. After a lot of social research and the invention of something called "MBA" it was decided that many aspects of this paternalism were mis-placed, that it made people too dependant on the company and, likewise, the company too dependent on a single group of workers. Change began to take place even before the Depression ended and World War II began. With unexpected swiftness the economy began to expand, jobs were going begging, and workers wanted a new deal of their own. There were jobs, but the cost of executing them began to grow. After the war labor and management seemed to pick up where they had left off in the pre-war years, each trying to get the most for the least, as it were. Enter the MBA.

Now we found we had a group of brainy folks who could count beans as well as people, and come up with something called "the bottom line." Sort of where the rubber meets the rhodium. Erase a line, increase a number. Add a line, remove a coin. Simple. Soon the counters were counting beans and forgetting the bean pickers. A penny saved on a $1,000 product translated into millions of pennies in a company's profit column. Soon it occurred to the folks in the front office that maybe it wasn't such a good idea to own all of the resources, or to have everything "on the shelf." After all, the government taxed inventory each year, and that certainly could put a dent in the salary bottom line. So the MBAs got busy again, looking at ways to cut inventory.

Once they started looking, it became possible to develop a model that would place all of the component parts and services on a time line, and organize them much like a freight yard organizes railroad cars: each car attached behind the engine in the sequence in which it would later be dropped off for loading/unloading. If you look at a freight yard from the air it looks somewhat like a playoff table for a basketball tournament. Eventually the lines all come together in a single train. So it appeared on the flow charts of the manufacturing geniuses in Detroit, I guess. Over the next few years the system went into place in a lot of industries, not just auto manufacturing. If the parts are made by other companies it is called "outsourcing." The ultimate extension of this, of course, is the increasingly common practice of outsourcing everything, including the workers.

And so we finally get to the part about my car. It wasn't a very serious problem: the air conditioning had been going down-hill for about a year, and finally, this June, it just gave up. After being in the shop for most of a day the specialist reported that the system needed three parts, including a hose. "We have everything but the hose. We'll have to get that from Baltimore but that will be here overnight." Have you heard that before? Do you know what that means? It means that the manufacturer has decided that unless there is a constant flow of parts from manufacturer to vehicle, they only order them when there is a need. Original parts are on a schedule so that they arrive on the assembly line when it is time to install them. For replacement parts it means the warehouse keeps only enough to resupply a scientifically determined number of requests, adjusted for who knows what. It's called "Just In Time."

Which brings us back to the car. I left it on a Monday evening, and when I finally was told that it would be ready, it was the following Monday afternoon. When I arrived at the shop to pay the ransom, I was told that the hose had only arrived on Friday afternoon, and that the car was still not completely assembled—that it would still need testing and probably wouldn't be ready until the next day. I wasn't pleased, but frankly, I wasn't surprised either. If a shop that is established for the repair and replacement of a manufacturer's products can't keep simple parts on hand, and if overnight delivery turns into three days, it is unrealistic to expect a mechanic to deliver his services on a schedule any more timely than that.

Anyway, after I examined the situation in depth with the service department manager, the car, now tested and repaired, I left the dealer's shop. It was late afternoon, nine days after I brought it in. And I had learned something: "just in time" really means just in time for the mechanic to go home.

About Invention

The first time I saw a machine that could take a tree and turn it into firewood "untouched by human hands," I was smitten. It's a fascinating piece of machinery that I recall with envy each time I approach the pile of un-cut, un-split trees at the top of my driveway. Of course the investment I already have in chain saws, mauls and related gear is sufficient for most homeowners, and I have told myself for years that the exercise is just what I need. Still, the machine appeals to me on several levels.

Anyway, while I was undergoing some physical therapy at the local muscle and tendon repair place in Monterey, I had time to give some thought to what kinds of machines we use in our lives, and how they came to be.

Most people who have looked at the history of invention would explain the better mouse trap syndrome in economic terms. The chain saw, for instance, is a replacement for at least one man on every two-man saw used in the big woods. Of course, I have seen some of the early chain saws and if they were operated by one man, Paul Bunyan lived. One saw, run by one man, could pile up sawdust faster than any two man whipsaw ever operated, so of course it gained in popularity and soon replaced the man-saw everywhere.

Many other inventions can trace their origins, at least on the surface, to a desire to do more with less: more product with less cost, more output with less energy. And therein lies what I believe to be the true driver behind invention: expending less energy. In other words, laziness.

Think of that father of all inventions, the Better Mouse Trap. Is there a cost to catching and disposing of the little creatures that demands economy of any sort? Not really. I've been in some places in the world where the little guys were considered a delicacy, served roasted or fried on a stick by street vendors. Now if you are going to use them as food, snapping them in traps isn't very productive. If you want to rid an area of them, killing one at a time isn't very economical. And think of the work involved in going out and actually snaring or shooting something as small as a mouse. Why it takes a bucket full just to make one meal! In fact, it is just too much effort to go out and bump-off a bunch of mice. Enter the mouse trap: quick, efficient, and it operates on its own without any batteries or fuel of any sort. Don't tell me about bait, either. I have some traps that haven't been baited in three or four years, but they keep on snapping over warm bodies year after year.

Anyway, the point here is how we have developed so many inventions simply because we were too lazy to get out there and do whatever it was that needed to be done. Take the car, for instance: it replaced the horse not because it was more reliable, or easier to operate, but because it took less time to maintain, or clean-up after. With a century of refinement it has become a little more reliable than the horse, but only a little. (Of course we are now realizing just how much we have to clean up after the car, but that's another story, isn't it?)

Which leads me to the next level: the "why haven't they invented…." part. For instance, why haven't they invented boomerang fencing? The way that would work would be that when the road hunters and other visitors threw their trash out along your road, it would hit the fence, and then relying on that well remembered law of physics, that for every action there is an equal and opposite reaction, the fence would catch the trash and return it from whence it came, i.e.; the window of the car.

Or how about vacuum baseboards? These would be attached to a central vac system and every time your dog walked through the room the vacuum would draw the dog hair and other detritus to the edge of the room and away.

And for those of us who live with trees, who could resist the rain gutter that has a trap-door bottom. Just operate a lever or an electronic remote control, and the hinged bottom would drop, dump the accumulated leaves, and then just as quickly close and be ready for the next rain.

Car owners, perhaps, would appreciate some combination of the baseboard and gutter arrangement, but I doubt that the Styrofoam fast food boxes and drink cans or bottles would be collected. Still, it does present a picture doesn't it: a car drives down the road, its vacuum-baseboard/drop-bottom gutter system sucking trash from the car, blowing it out on the roadside where the boomerang fencing shoots it back into the vehicle. But maybe that is the answer for those who think drive-by trashing is okay. A sort of "what goes around comes around" moment.

About Monsters

Monsters have been around a long time. I took note of it originally in this essay from 2001.

I read a newspaper story the other day in which a man identified as chief investment strategist for a major brokerage firm, said: "Unemployment claims have been dropping like a stone over the past two months. They haven't been this low since early 1989." Now that, it seemed to me, was good news. Not so, according to the expert. "Put it all together," he went on, "and there's another, big, nasty employment report in our future."

Now what did this man mean by that statement? Was he expecting the unemployment rate to suddenly shoot upward? Not at all. Instead he and his fellow toilers among the paper pushers are expecting the nation's central bank, known as "the Fed," to raise interest rates. Presumably that is a bad thing because it probably reflects itself in terms of raising the interest a man like this would have to pay on the loan for his next Porsche.

So I wonder what kind of men are these that they can sit in a Wall Street tower and bemoan the fact that the people on the sidewalk have jobs? Isn't that what the politicians have been promising ever since the beginning? How does a man get to the point where he can look at rising employment as something to be avoided? Perhaps this man and his ilk have not walked to work in New York or any other major American city in the last few decades. I rather suspect that the limos can get right to the door at his place of business (better not to call it a place of employ…well, I probably shouldn't use the "e" word in writing about these people) and the occupants can scurry across ten or so feet of sidewalk, protected from the sight, sound and smell of the branch of the unemployed who call the street home.

One other thing they worry about when the numbers are going down: the competition for workers increases the cost of labor. It is part of what we were taught was the law of supply and demand. That's the competitive marketplace at work, you see. When something is scarce it has more value than when supply is high and demand is scarce. Is there something wrong with that? Well it is only good if you are selling a product, but not if you are selling your labor.

But it is all numbers on paper anyway. When wages rise, prices rise. When prices rise interest rises. When interest rises banks and credit companies encourage you to spend the future by saying things like "it will never be cheaper." When demand drops, of course, these same people encourage you to buy "as a hedge against inflation."

Don't misunderstand me. I don't believe in "make work" jobs for anyone. I do believe that people have to be flexible today, as downsizing and reinventing flash through the various corporate consulting firms. I also believe that everyone physically capable of working should do so, even if it pays no more than the rent. We used to talk about the dignity of labor. Where else will people learn what that means, except in the workplace?

Many years ago, when the automobile industry was first looking at computer-driven automation, a labor leader said that he had no objection to machines in the workplace, but "who," he asked, "will buy the Fords?" He was talking about the prospect of machines making machines, replacing human hands and muscle, but the ultimate effect is the same:

unemployed workers are not strong consumers. Alfred P. Sloan Jr, president and, later, chairman of General Motors, envisioned a global future of increasing consumerism, and directed his corporation to create demand, even as it created product: Chevrolet for the man on his way up, a Cadillac for the man at the top, and two or three plateaus in between. You could measure a family's success by the car in the driveway. But Sloan understood that he couldn't sell his cars to people without jobs.

Today machines do make Chevys and Fords. Who makes the monsters?

Part III—Window Seat

The American Century

I wrote this in July of 1999, when the drumbeat for the millennium was already strong.

I'm not exactly sure when we began to think of this as "The American Century," but I do know that it has gone on long enough that at least two, perhaps three generations are convinced of the rightness of that title.

We have tended to think that because we own most of the world's wealth, more of its luxuries, certainly more than a necessary share of the methods of total annihilation we are not just invincible, we are IN CHARGE.

We rule the skies, the waves, the fields. American scientists and inventors have decanted a cornucopia of tools and toys into the world's hands. Not without some losses, to be sure, yet here we are, at the end of "our" century, still in control; still the leader. Isn't it wonderful?

Well, let's look at what we really have done. Certainly the hands and minds of America have reshaped the world my grandparents knew. Farms produce more per acre because we invented the tools and the ways of building more of them. Factories churn out more goods at lower cost than ever before, thanks to American management philosophies as much as to American ingenuity. People everywhere have access to information because of the invention and development of the telephone, the telegraph, radio, tv, computers; all American, and all given universal application during this century—the American century.

And we have demonstrated a way of life envied by almost every culture on earth. We live in houses with indoor plumbing and outdoor stoves (a really interesting reversal of the past, if you ask me). Our children can go to school for years and years, gradually rising to exalted titles and positions (even if they do lack the skills for survival). Our elderly can (at least for the present) count on a financial program that will see them through their "golden" years (if they don't get sick). We've even developed a financial system that can "fine tune" the economy by just thinking about changing interest rates. There have been so many advances. What's missing?

This summer should bring us to our senses. It has certainly been an attack on them. While all the world is marveling at our techno-superiority, or wishing they were as good, we are being reminded that no matter how strong our military, how detailed our planning, how righteous our causes, we still have failures. We can't always locate our enemies, or hit the targets, or tell friend from foe. Mistakes are made.

On the home front, every group has its champion, every persuasion its group. No one need feel left out (or included in) unless he (or she) wants in (or out). We have taken each new idea as a challenge, every philosophical direction as a commandment. We can make resources disappear or conserve them depending on the color of our national mood ring. People and opinions can be changed or molded as rapidly as positions are defined. We can develop new materials, design new techniques, preserve life beyond the biblical three-score and ten while we are finding better and better ways of putting a stop to huge chunks of life at a single flash.

We can rule the seas and skies (to an extent), but we still are subject to the will of the next tornado, the next hurricane. We are still helpless in stopping nature from doing what it wants. I ask you: If this is the American Century, why can't we control the weather?

About Government

This was written in 2001, but little has changed in the decade since, except personally: I have come to embrace the internet, and even e-mail.

In the 1980's we heard a lot about "getting government off our backs." Unfortunately we didn't hear the rest of the coda: "...and into our living rooms and bedrooms." Now we are at a pretty pass. Unregulated businesses like airlines are making life more unpleasant for the majority, the urge to grab has taken over every sector of the economy, and the government is indeed in our homes.

This summer the Supreme Court will be offering a judgement on what can and cannot be available over the Internet. Like so many intrusions into our lives, both the "net" and the government hold the prospect of serving the greater good. Just who that good is for is in question.

It isn't for me, because even though I have used computers for years, and can get excited about advances in technology, I have (without too much effort) resisted e-mail and the Internet without regret. I do have friends who prefer to correspond that way, and surely there is some utility in having the world's knowledge at your fingertips, especially for a writer or researcher, but not for me. I will stick to the tried and true (and slow) methods of finding information: use the library, the encyclopedia, identify and interview experts, educate myself as much as possible on the subject through standard texts and publications, and then make up my own mind. I'm afraid that if I asked a question on the Internet and, as a friend on the faculty at a nearby college did, received some eight-thousand replies, I'd just give up the project altogether.

But all of that distracts from my main theme: guarding ourselves from ourselves.

When I read or hear about an art exhibition or a sculpture display that deals with something that, to me, is disgusting, or presents something of poor taste and low morals, I just don't go see it. I make that judgement myself. If it is a question of a minor child being exposed, and the child is mine, I exercise parental authority and leadership and "just say no." That is where the responsibility lies, not with the courts or the congress or any group, ultra-liberal, libertarian or ultra conservative. (How close those three are in outlook is disconcerting enough on the surface.)

Now the real question in my mind is why anyone would wish the government, at any level, to have the authority and responsibility for telling me or my children and grandchildren what we can see or do or say? Which government? The one that sits in Washington spending money for private constituents? The one that can't get down to the business of governing because it is spending millions of dollars a year on investigations of itself? The one that accuses one side of doing what the other has already done? Just who are these people that we can watch them take money from vested interests ranging from various rights activists to foreign governments and then expect them to be Solomon-like in their deliberations about abortion, education, Internet and television programming, and all of the many other things we want government to do? In other words, how can we expect our morals to be legislated when the legislators are so busy defending themselves against moral turpitude?

Are we listening? Does Washington listen?

About The ABC Murders—The death of education in America

Once again we read about the desire to tinker with the educational system, this time (2010) in a major school system where non-educators want to mess with the curriculum, deleting subjects such as Evolution, and Thomas Jefferson. This essay was written in 1997.

At somewhat irregular intervals it seems, some individual or organization mounts an attack on the American educational system in what they, at least, feel is a genuine effort to correct some wrong or redress some imbalance. It doesn't matter whether it is an attempt to expunge prayer from the schools (or return it to its former importance), remove or replace a form of punishment, or establish some curriculum consistent with an individual's own view of the world. What is important, it seems to me, is what it does to the educational system itself, and therefore, to future generations of citizens. Case in point, as Rod Serling was wont to say, is the current move to guarantee everyone the right to two years of college.

When my father was growing up he attended public schools in Philadelphia and New York City. His formal schooling was completed after 11 years, the standard for the time (he was born in January, 1900). Yet even when I was graduating from high school in North Carolina, in the early 50's, after 12 years of mandatory education, I was already less educated than he. My sister, who was four years ahead of me, was in the last class meeting a state requirement for Latin, for instance. There was not even a foreign language requirement by the time I graduated, except for one year of Spanish or French in junior high school (now called "middle," though it is not book-ended by an equal number of school years). Our father had studied Latin as well as Greek, knew history and algebra, and wrote in a fine, slanting script acceptable to even the most critical of calligraphers. Surely in a generation the expansion of knowledge hadn't been so accelerated that not only was another year required for mastery, but some basic subjects had to be withheld! Yet that is what happened.

Yes, my father's generation witnessed the exchange of horsepower for fossil fuel power, and grew up with manned flight, poison gas and aerial bombardment. But none of those things were taught in detail in primary education. Something else was happening.

Many communities moved from one-room, one-teacher, multi-grade schools to consolidated, multi-teacher institutions. There were other needs to be met as social programs took children out of the workplace and into the school room. Parents left the home and entered the work shop. Soon the schools were being used for more than just education.

In my father's generation such schools were generally limited to cities and large towns. By my generation that was hardly an option. Government began to intrude as the representative of people outside the school district, and some semblance of national standards began to be discussed. Just as today there is concern that students be able to use knowledge to advance themselves, there was, from our nation's inception, a realization that education was important. The founding fathers, I think, understood that an educated population was less easily bamboozled by dictators and other false prophets, better able to separate fact from fiction, more likely to make decisions affecting their community and country based on understanding, not simply emotional appeal.

What happened? Children left the workplace (farm or factory) for the classroom, and parents left the home to replace them. Mom and Dad gave up a measure of control that carried with it the responsibility for guiding, leading and teaching those principles and practices that, when combined with knowledge, allowed people to made judgements and decisions based in ethics and morals necessary to the preservation of democracy. Is that too far-fetched?

Today schools are care-takers (though not very good ones if you look at drug use, teen sex and gang violence in so many schools across the nation). At the same time the school must apply rules to teachers and staff that prevent them doing anything constructive or forceful by way of teaching consequences. Respect and responsibility, those twin strands of the DNA of society, aren't part of the basic curricula. When I was growing up I learned that "no" meant "no." Not just to questions about sex or alcohol, but to everyday things like taking without permission something that wasn't yours, or saying that you had (or had not) done something you were supposed to have done (or not done). We didn't learn it by rote, either. We learned it by example from parents and teachers. If you were told "no" about something, regardless of by whom, that was that. "Never take no for an answer," was something a salesman had to learn, but that wasn't applicable to questions of morality and righteousness.

Anyway, we have now watered down the educational system to the extent that students graduate without being able to read, do simple math or speak a coherent and precise tongue. "Whatever." And along comes a proposal to guarantee a two-year college education. What for? If we can't prepare people in

12 years, what difference will two years make? Surely the "requirements" for graduation will include more of the same nonsense now visited on children in 12 years of primary education. If we are going to do that why not just extend high school two years? It just doesn't make any sense to me to add another layer in the hope that it will fix the twelve previous years.

It is all too reminiscent of a bumper sticker popular about ten years ago: if at first you don't succeed, lower your standards!

A Super Natural Event

The Christmas gift catalogues are beginning to arrive in the mail, and here, in the frontier settlement of Head Waters, they are a welcome link to the outside world.

When we sit here on our mountainside, we have ample opportunity to observe the world immediately around us, and to learn from the exhibits which nature provides on a daily basis. Each morning brings new shading and illumination to the fields and mountains that are our ever-changing landscape. Birds and squirrels, deer and rabbits, chipmunks and opossum, as well as the odd bear and our own dogs provide an endless source of pleasure, knowledge and entertainment.

Elsewhere I have commented on the birds we observe here, and how we are trying to understand nature from the perspective of former city-dwellers. What sparks this new observation is something that one of the catalogs has brought to my attention. Now before I describe the item, I must prepare you a little.

First, I think there is much to learn from observing the world around us, especially about such things as getting along with others in a symbiotic framework. When we talk about observing nature, we generally mean those things one gleans from some encounter, perhaps with an animal or a plant or a sunset. It is an active, not a passive state, and one which you often must pursue in order to gain any insight. There are times, of course, when we are simply brought face-to-face quite accidentally with something that is of incredible beauty, or that is normally beyond our understanding, and we receive sudden bursts of vision into the core of the world around us. But for the most part our learning is from observation first hand.

Second, even the city dweller may observe the natural world and the works therein, and make connections with the larger world. There are parks, roof tops, even back yard gardens in which one may sit quietly and observe and learn.

Nature programs on television are interesting, perhaps, but not quite the same as being there. The response one feels in the face of such things is along the lines of "really, how interesting," but seldom, for me at least, a sort of "ah, ha!" recognition of a revelation. That we reserve for something we have truly learned directly.

And what has this to do with Christmas catalogs? Well, I'm always bemused by the juxtaposition of bird houses and rodent traps, squirrel feeders and ultrasonic deer repellents: in short, ways in which one may attract and at the same time, defeat, the natural world we profess to love. Yes, there are places where certain animals are not welcome, or where one would like to have them but only when it is convenient, but the total double-sidedness of the retailers is perhaps what gets me.

Anyway, one crop of catalogs offered something that I just couldn't resist bringing to your attention, as an example of something truly at odds with my own concept of nature study. It is a video camera small enough to mount on a bird feeder, so that you can observe and hear your feathered visitors on your television set. Our livingroom windows are just like giant tv screens, and we can sit and watch with some invisibility what goes on in the trees and on the ground before us. We can glance up and see a hawk pair soaring out over the fields, we can take a foreshortened view and watch a squirrel casually slip out on the high wire that holds a feeder, we can even look at the deck immediately beyond the door and watch the little birds make track prints in the snow.

I'm not sure what it is, exactly, that bothers me about using an electronic spying device to see a bird feeding, but somehow it just doesn't feel right. Perhaps it is the limit it puts on our view, and our understanding. Like all spying perhaps, this reveals only the immediate and the nearby. There is no environment, no context. The foreground and background may be fuzzy and out of focus, which is the nature of a close-up lens, as any photographer can tell you. It is, perhaps, the difference between history and recall: one is a study of the recorded facts, long after the events and the participants are gone. The other is what individual pairs of eyes observed, what emotions were evoked, what responses were given. As I think about it, I guess that what really bothers me about watching a bird through a fixed, narrow point of view is that it only reveals what is happening immediately, and has no breadth of understanding or depth of enlightenment.

It is the CNN view of life.

Beware of Wolves

In 1997, our small county (population 2,300 and shrinking) was suddenly under siege. The military flying services had decided that our nearly uninhabited county would be wonderful for testing "nap-of-the-earth (300 foot altitude)" skills, and our water was suddenly deemed unfit for fish. Meetings were held...

Just about the time you think you can sit down and let the world go by, along comes another happy experiment in government. If we aren't being flattened by the Air Force, the DEQ is piling another load of something on our shoulders. Then, mysteriously, someone at the EPA (a kind of neighborhood watch operated by federal busybodies) decides Strait Creek is on the endangered list. If you weren't there you missed the best show in town, when Monterey took on the state water control board.

At about the time that meeting took place, the Air Force took the proposal to expand training flights "off the table" (their term), admitting they had failed to do their homework regarding Highland County. What they really discovered, however, was that we were not exactly the voiceless, faceless few whom they could barely see, even at 300 feet.

Both of these incidents point up something very rich and rewarding about being a part of a county like Highland. We, as a community, are articulate, knowledgeable, and most importantly, we are staunch defenders of our place and way of life.

Having been one of the many county residents concerned about the DEQ's action, I attended both the first public meeting, and the subsequent Water Control Board hearing. That was the meeting where our freedoms were blatantly abridged by the state representatives who decided what could be presented and what was forbidden. All the more remarkable, then, was the presentation led by one of our retirees, and so admirably filled out by all of his associates. I think what surprised the Water Control Board panel more than anything was the depth of scientific knowledge and experience invested in those who presented Highland's case. It was truly impressive.

For the record, the issue has attracted a lot of support from around the state, as evidenced by a visit recently from the state Secretary of the Department of Environmental Quality, as well as attendance at the hearing by our State Senator and local Delegate. The town still may lose on points of law, but at least the residents have found and twisted the nose of the otherwise faceless bureaucracy in Richmond.

As for the Air Force, that really drew a reaction! Everyone had an opinion, and many of us put our names to petitions and letters demanding reconsideration. In the end every one of our elected representatives: the governor, senators and representatives all took up the cry. What is important in both of these issues, it seems to me, is not just that we "won" something, but that we raised our voices (with true Southern comity and grace) to a pitch and level that caused powerful people to listen, and to act.

Now compare that with the action and attitude of the members of the Water Control Board. Here was an administrative arm of the executive branch making rules, enforcing the rules they have made, and then determining who is in compliance and finally, setting the punishment of those who fail. Not a pretty picture.

All of this brings to mind the issue of garbage. I began to wonder if that had not been the real "watershed" issue. When the state determined that water they could not find was seeping through holes they could not locate into the Jackson River in a way they could not demonstrate, instead of concluding that our landfill was a tight and secure one, ordered us to make a bigger sacrifice than we can easily afford. The landfill is now closed, and instead of not polluting the Jackson, we are now sending our garbage out of the county where, eventually, it will end up in some scow towed out to sea, where it will probably be dumped under cover of darkness in someone else's waters. There have been numerous stories in the last decade of garbage scows from Hell condemned to be towed back and forth over the seas until, like displaced persons after World War II, they could either find a government that could be shamed into accepting them, or they made an illegal landing in a place like Israel. Otherwise they simply sank without a trace.

As I recall the story, the supervisors did the best they could, given the low turnout at hearings to discuss the problem, and the lack of expression of community concern and involvement. The consequence (the trash tax) has awakened us to our responsibilities as citizens, I think, and we will not let that happen again.

All of this has been a lesson in democracy and freedom other communities would do well to learn. Those who are elected and appointed to serve us could perhaps pick up a thought or two, as well. I commend to those charged with governing us, these words from Thomas Jefferson: "Cherish, therefore, the spirit of the people, and keep alive their attention. Do not be too severe upon their errors, but reclaim them by enlightening them. If once they become inattentive to public affairs, you and I, Congress and Assemblies, Judges and Governors, shall all become wolves."

A New Bird

This was written not so long ago, but long enough that a first class stamp was still 33 cents (and recently enough that there is not a "cent" symbol on my keyboard).

I hadn't really noticed before, but when I added a one-cent stamp to the envelope, to make up for the change in first class postage, I realized that the penny stamp I was using pictures a bird. And not just any bird, but an American Kestrel. Elsewhere among these essays you will read my description of an attack on a blue jay by just such a bird, here in front of our house. It was an interesting contest between two birds of equal size, but one in which the Kestrel had all the advantages, despite the fact that there was a whole covey of jays watching.

What the stamp brought to mind were thoughts of the US Postal Service, and other moves over the years to "privatize" the government. Efforts to cut loose some of the established government agencies, of course, have been balanced by taking under the government's wing, so to speak, such things as the passenger rail service. The post office, of course, was one of the first government services (after the military and Customs) established by those revolutionaries in Philadelphia.

I must say that the postal service has taken on all of the aspects of a private business, even though, of course, it couldn't operate without its very cozy relationship with the bureaucracy and, certainly, Congress. In truth, it is still a government agency, and as such has most of the hallmarks of that association. It can't for instance, operate at a profit. That isn't just because of the way it operates, but also because it isn't allowed by law. Which should give you a good feeling about this most important service Benjamin Franklin brought to life in the hope that it would improve communications, as well as trade, among the several states and with other governments.

I don't always understand it, but I think that element (improved relations with other countries) must have been what was behind the USPS sponsorship of a bicycle racer in the 2000 Tour de France. Now, I admit that seeing the yellow jersey on an American rider was a nice thing, and I have a great deal of admiration for the young man who wore it, but I'm still trying to figure out why the US Postal Service saw that as promoting the use of what is so often referred to these days as "snail mail." It seems not quite apt, to me.

Still, some motion here must be relevant, otherwise why would an organization so in debt that it has to raise prices, be spending the kind of money reportedly spent on a guy on a bike? As much as I admire those who compete in bike racing, I am not certain I want to support it financially. There are so many other ways my money could be re-cycled. Or is that what they mean when they say, "what goes around comes around?"

Anyway, I have about used up my stock of 33-cent stamps, and when they are gone, the one-cent variety will be, too. I'll miss it. Even though it is a predator, it is handsome and effective. It's just that I have felt a little less enthusiasm for the US Postal Service, ever since they gave us the bird.

Part IV—Fellow Travelers

Message From a Mouse

One difference between the country and the city is the relationships one can establish with small beings of all persuasions. Winged ones are the ones we notice mostly—birds and bugs—because they are either the most visible, or the most annoying.

The little creatures that walk are for some reason more difficult to notice and observe. So when one allows itself to be seen, it is an even more rewarding experience. There is always the temptation, of course, to assign human characteristics to them, perhaps as a way of observing and understanding them.

Chipmunks, for instance, will hold my attention for as long as they are in sight. There are a few that live under the deck on the front of our house, primarily, I suspect, for the sunflower seeds I put out for the birds. For some reason I am much more tolerant of the chipmunks than of the squirrels. Perhaps it is because the chippies eat and run. The squirrel is more inclined to linger and stuff his face, sitting in the dish that hangs from a tree.

Oh, yes, it is true that squirrels are great acrobats. And smart, too. I've tried most designs of squirrel-proof feeders, and I can tell you this: a squirrel proof designation simply means "against one squirrel at a time." It only takes a couple of attempts at one of those feeders that closes down when the weight of any thing larger than a blue jay gets on it before the squirrel calls for help. Then, while one holds the gate open, the other reaches in and feeds! And have you ever moved a feeder after watching a squirrel make what seems to be an effortless leap from ground to station? Or drop from tree branch to feeder top? Move it and observe what happens. After one failed attempt, the squirrel goes back to the starting line, and you can almost hear the synapses snapping as he calculates the distance, wind, weight and degree of hunger before leaping again—and landing within striking distance. Maybe by one paw, or a tail's wrap, but he's there, eating away.

The chipmunk, on the other hand, locates the source, dashes in, fills his cheek pouches, and then runs away. He will return as often as he can, body and legs in clockwork mechanical motion, tail moving in metronomic arcs, as close to a wind-up toy as you can get. Certainly this little fellow could have been the inspiration for those early makers of clockwork toys that gave so much pleasure at the beginning of the mechanical age.

But the animal I most admire is the mouse. Here in the country mice are a different breed from the ones city dwellers know, I'm sure of that. First of all, they are mostly outdoor types. They live in barns and other outbuildings where fresh grains, old hay, and green growing things provide a healthy diet. Even storage buildings and garages attract them because these are much easier to enter and leave than a well sealed house, especially if there are dogs or cats living there. Mice will find a comfortable place, locate materials and make a proper home in anything that isn't used regularly. I'm always amazed (and amused) at where and how these little folks use space.

The first time I encountered a mouse's creativity was when I opened the hood of my car and found a nest carefully built on top of the heater box. Of course the mouse was no longer there, probably frightened away soon after she moved in the first time I started the engine, but the signs were there, along with the half eaten insulation around the heater. My wife's car has proven such an attraction to the garage mice that I've had to start trapping them routinely. A mouse trap sits on the garage floor under the engine, and I catch one every few months. It is there because the mice have discovered that they can get from the floor into the air cleaner intake tube, which lies beside the left front wheel. The first time I found that they had been in there was when I was changing the air filter. When I pulled the old one out, I discovered about a pound of shelled acorns neatly stacked in the filter box. It was tempting to make jokes about "the nut beside the wheel," and about the car depending on well fed mice for power, but the car ran better after I removed the stash, so I now conduct mouse checks as part of the regular maintenance program.

I have found nests in drawers, flower pots, tool boxes, old tires, tractor engine compartments and on shelves: almost anywhere things are stored and not used frequently. In one building I found a big nest on the end of a shelf. For some time I left it there, but finally one day I decided it was time for the mouse family to move on. I removed the nest. I put some mouse traps out. A few days later I checked the building and found both traps were still set, but the cheese was gone. And the traps had been carefully moved to one place. The mouse was clearly telling me that he was on to my game. I reset the traps and left the building. The next time I went to the shed the traps were where I had placed them, unmolested. The mice had obviously hit the road.

But there was one final message from the head mouse: on the tractor seat was a neat pile of nuts!

Birds

The burble of the telephone reached me as I walked into the living room. On the second ring I picked it up, and began talking. Simultaneously, another musical sound entered my consciousness. Outside, beyond the large glass doors, birds, many birds, were in full-throated cry. I asked the caller if she could hear the sound, and held the receiver near the screen. She could, and wondered what was causing such a choral outburst, for it was obvious that every bird around was involved in this songfest. A storm, I speculated, for it was a July afternoon, when thunderstorms are not uncommon. The dogs know, and show they are upset, so maybe it is the same with the birds, I offered.

Finally I spotted several of the birds. Bluejays, I announced. A lot of them. They were full into their alarm song when I noticed something on the ground. There. Ten or fifteen feet beyond the edge of the wide deck. Something brownish, moving slightly on the ground. I stepped outside, and walked to the edge of the deck, still holding the phone, describing what I could see for my caller: a brownish bird, not bigger than a jay. The bird's actions seemed those of one either hurt or pretending to be, in order to drive away a predator.

A brownish bird, with bars across the tail. A hawk, said my friend. It must be a Kestrel. It was then that I saw, beneath the bird's outstretched wings, a jay. Immobilized by the brown bird's talons, covered by its wings. So that is what the noise is all about. A predator has made a capture, and the other jays are screaming in anger and fear. As I watched, the hawk moved his prey slightly, trying to get it away. It was too big to carry, so whatever was going to be done had to be done here, where they were. The jay was passive, giving no hint of struggle. Was it already lifeless, I wondered?

I ended the conversation as I went inside to get a camera. By the time I returned, still attaching the 135 mm lens, the prey was gone. I had approached within ten feet before going back to the house, and now the whole thing seemed over. But the jays were still calling, though they seemed to be further down the slope that lay between the house and the road.

Following their calls, I came to the edge, and there, a few yards to my right, I saw again the little hawk. Time for one quick, probably poor shot, and then, when I looked back after making an adjustment to the camera, the bird was gone.

On the walk back up the slope to the house, I looked at the area where I had first seen the bird on the ground. No feathers, no bones, no blood. Nor had there been any at the edge of the slope where I had last seen the hawk and heard the jays. It had been only a few minutes long, it may not have been as detailed as the edited scenes shown on television, but it was real; something happened before my eyes that may not be witnessed soon again. But it could be re-run in my mind, where it was now stored forever.

A Management Theory For The Birds

I didn't grow up knowing the names of trees or birds or butterflies. So when I moved to the country, I had to learn them when my mind was already full of a lifetime. I have become an observer, but my terms of reference are of the city man's view of life; of the city in the last half of the 20th century, when contention, strife, confrontation are the calls of the wild. In such terms do I look at birds.

When I have breakfast in the mornings I share it with the flock. It's much like a coffee break in the employees' lounge except that in the winter I am on the inside. The table is before one of the 8-foot wide glass doors that make up much of the south face of our house. The birds congregate at three hanging feeders, or picnic on the ground. One group this winter has been the executive council: Evening grosbeaks, in their gold and black overcoats, gather around a 12" dish that hangs from a tree limb. It is obvious that these are the drivers, the powerhouses of the organization. Even as they exchange places, fly off to chivvy some of the younger finches and nuthatches that dart in and away from the trees and tube feeders, or drop down to one of the picnic groups, all carry the same concern with the state of the organization. They gather around the circle, nod, grumble, peck at their food, puff themselves up, eat and go back to whatever grosbeaks do when they aren't eating.

On the other feeders are the staff; the office drones and wannabirds (they can't be wanna-bees). Power-hungry, they dive in and out, pushing less aggressive members off the perches, grabbing what they can, in turn being forced to take flight themselves.

The juncos are the labor pool. When I am late in the morning, or when the demand for food has been particularly high, a crisis develops at the feeding stations: they need refilling, and I haven't yet been out to do my job. Then I can expect an angry delegation from among the juncos, marching up the broad wooden steps of the deck, then boldly crossing the five-foot wide upper deck to the glass door opposite where I sit. A little foot-stomping is all I need to motivate me to bring the feed. If I don't get the seed out fast enough I will have at least one air-pounding overflight close to my head when I do. As soon as I'm on my way back to the deck, the feeders are filled with birds, not a few tossing off a final birdie expletive in my direction. So much for thanks. It's almost like being back in the office. I might even get an additional show of muscle once I'm back inside, as two or three grey-overcoated, fedora wearing, cigar smoking juncos parade nonchalantly past the glass door, spitting seed shells onto the wood.

Having been a boss for many years, and having had to deal with employee demands and what they believed were their rights, I can live with the relatively benign behavior of these birds. The trouble is, it can get brutal.

We've tried the predator cut-outs that keep the birds from flying into large windows. We have baskets hanging from the soffit. Nothing works. It took me a while to figure it out, of course, because I'm neither an industrial psychologist nor an experienced nature-watcher. When I look at tracks in the snow, I see tracks in the snow, not where a hawk swooped down and grabbed a mouse, or a coyote followed a fawn. Just tracks. So when I first began picking broken birds off the deck I simply assumed that these were among the more nearsighted. Perhaps just the lonely ones, seeking like the dog Aesop tells us about, to make friends with their own reflection. But I have finally come to understand the sequence of events, and the motivation behind it.

It only happens when the feeders are empty. It is always around the same time of morning; and they are almost always juncos. Sometimes it may escalate to a nuthatch or finch, but not the grosbeaks or the cardinals. Not even a jay has ever breached the invisible barrier of the decks and steps. Just those beefy, grey-coated guys who march on me occasionally when I am late with the food, or the mid-level folks with fancy titles and colorful coats. That's when it happens.

From among the big boys at the roundtable the word goes down. Along the chain of command, the middle managers and office staffs carry the message: if you expect to keep eating at this table, you must sacrifice! For that is what it is. A chosen one to make the ultimate gift to the lord of the feed bucket. A gift so that the others may continue their endless occupation of feeding and flying and feeding again. It's a sacrifice. They fly against the glass when I'm not just late, but darned late; when I am not even visible at my usual place at the table. A sudden, loud "thump," and the bird falls to the deck.

It's what the theorists might call management by objection.

Field Work

In the Spring of 2001, life was still regulated by such simple pleasures as a break-of-day ramble.

We really look forward to our mornings in the fields, the dogs and I. Usually we are out sometime after sunrise, often before the sun clears the mountain that marks our southeastern border. By the time we have covered the course around the two fields, the sun is visible, and the northwestern edges of the fields are in strong sun. It is a wonderful time of day, when the dew (or frost) is still on the ground, and the birds are just beginning their morning songs.

We leave the house and go along the gravel drive, the dogs running ahead. When we get to the turn, where the drive goes down to the county road, all three usually take a quick run up the mountain on our western border, after some laughing squirrel or other, before giving up and following me down the drive. About a hundred yards along is the gate to the fields. Between the end of the driveway and the gate are all sorts of morning signs: hoof and paw prints, droppings, rubbings which must all be investigated and marked before entering the field.

Of the 100-plus acres of this mountain farm, only about 25 are cleared. In the past we have had chickens and hogs and sheep, as well as a flock of geese, but now we share our land only with those that were here before us, large and small. Deer mice and deer, opossum and raccoon, gray rabbit and black bear, all manner of things that burrow, bore, walk, slither and fly. Our morning walk takes us down the edge of the small field, clockwise around it, until we come back to our starting point, and head down to the river. Occasionally the dogs will take time to roll in the grass, sniff-out small animal burrows, and pay their respects to the rabbits who live in the brush along the edges.

Once we have circled the field and we reach the river, it is time for a drink (if the water isn't frozen), or a swim (if is isn't completely frozen). I take a moment to look for the fish that live under the bank, or among the fallen trees that have taken up places in the water. There are some deep pools where the small brownies congregate, and an occasional rainbow. The water remains friendly to trout year 'round.

Sometimes we'll surprise a family of brown ducks that visits in the Fall, or a blue heron. The other day some Canadas made a brief stop on their way North (it is now April). Each day brings something new to see and hear in our fields, and we never tire of taking the same trip, most days. If it is below about 20 degrees, breathing becomes a little unpleasant, and if it is raining hard or snowing I tend to keep indoors, but the dogs will, for the most part, do the walk any time.

As we enter the big field from the little copse of trees, we continue along the riverside, heading mostly into the sun. Occasionally, across the river, a deer or two will freeze in sudden awareness of our presence, but seldom do the dogs notice them, or if they do, know that I will call them in instantly should they attempt to cross the river and give chase. Some things are just not done!

On we go, following a well-worn path about seven feet wide; a path I keep trimmed with a small garden tractor. The rest of the field I cut once or twice a year with the big tractor, a job I look forward to, but quickly tire of, especially in late August or early September when the days are still hot and the fields are dusty. But keeping them cut is part of the stewardship of the land Besides, it justifies two tractors.

In the big field are mice, ground hogs, snakes and other objects of interest to the dogs. They take very seriously their responsibility for keeping things in check, or at least making a good show of it. All three are scent hunters, I think, and they keep their noses to the ground, hard at work until I get to the far end, and come around to the near side of the field. By now the sun has reached the path, and finding a sunny spot, I stop and hand out half a dog biscuit each. The other half is served when we arrive back at the house.

In the field, Bear, the Chow/Sheltie mix, shows his independence. While Killian the Collie, and Baby the Spaniel mix, can hardly contain themselves in anticipation of the treat, Bear often has to be coaxed to even come join the group. Independent, he will often sniff the treat, shake his head and walk away. He is the only dog I've ever known who would refuse a handout, even fresh meat from the hunter who keeps his camp in a small hollow next to us. Whatever the problems he faced as a puppy, it had something to do with being handed food, I think. Even though he and I have been boon companions for a decade, he will still sometimes refuse a treat from me. When we get back to the house it is different: he is as eager as the others to take his share.

As we continue up the field to get back to our starting point, the dogs will often begin to chase each other. As we get near the apple trees, Bear and Killian begin their dominance game (both being males), until Bear throws the larger Killian the requisite two out of three. Then we can continue up the trail, along the road and up the drive. Another day has begun.

Dancing With Dogs

In the years since this was written, all three of the dogs have left our lives, but not our memories. Their replacements have continued the tradition, but perhaps without the same elan.

Three dogs share their house with us. We are very thankful that they do, for otherwise our lives would be measurably less interesting and exciting, if somewhat less hairyed, if you know what I mean.

The largest of the three, and the middle one in terms of age, is the aristocrat of the pack. He is a long-haired collie, who answers (sometimes) to the name of "Killian." Many times, as befits a dog of great breeding and intelligence, he chooses not to hear you, which allows him the freedom to continue to explore or simply lie like a shag rug on the deck. Of course all dogs, like children, suffer from CLDD (chronic listening deficit disorder), which can recur at anytime and under any circumstance. Killian's usually overcomes him at 1 A.M., when it is time for bed and the world is quiet, and you have to stand outside and yell "Kil—li-annnn! C-o-o-o-me!" It comes without warning quite often, actually. A rabbit popping out of a hole, a leaf that blows across his field of vision, are just some of the things that trigger CLDD.

Sometimes he hears, but he focuses his attention on the echo coming off the opposite mountain. He looks in that direction, silently asking: "Who called?" There are other times when he hears, and I know it, and he knows I know it. Then he will look at me, get up and walk until my line of sight is blocked by a tree. This is where his intelligence falters. As large as he is, only he thinks he can't be seen. His large hindquarters and full tail, however, give him away every time.

Smallest and youngest is a spaniel mix, long haired, silky black and with deep, dark eyes. I know that she is a mix, because when she gets to water she only wants to put half of herself in it. We live by a river, which the other dogs find good for bathing even in the winter, but Baby will just stand at the edge and wet her nose. In the fields adjacent to the river, of course, she throws herself happily into any puddle, especially if it is muddy.

In the middle as judged by size, and the true leader of the pack, is Bear. He is a cross between a chow and a pointy-nosed something. When he was a puppy his whole tongue was black, but that has evolved into a spotted affair, still unmistakably chow. Except for a slightly longer snout, he retains other chow features, including the heavy coat and bushy tail he carries curled over his back like a scorpion's. Because of his coloring he is known as "the little red dog" to some of the folks who live along our road.

Now there are people who will tell you that dogs don't smile, that they can't really speak, and that they have no memory or sense of humor. Those folks don't live here. In fact, if they have only been exposed to some really laid back or job-focused dogs, they really haven't any concept of what a dog can do.

Like people, our three companions have very distinct personalities. All are easy to live with most of the time, and great fun to be with except when those strange invisible doggy satellites slip by overhead and all three begin to race from one end of the house to the other, barking in tuneless chorus at what only they know. Of course, it is their house, so it doesn't behoove us to ask, "Why are you barking?" more than once or twice before we quiet down. We don't always suggest that they stop because many times it is a form of visitor arrival announcement. The trouble is they may consider anyone on the road below our house to be a visitor. The barking stops abruptly when the car passes without coming up the drive. Of course if a family member has been away, even for an hour, they will begin barking as much as 30 minutes before whoever is away actually arrives home again. Somehow they receive a telepathic message about the time the traveler begins visualizing "home." That's not a dog-owner's speculation, by the way, but a rather well documented experience. Try it yourself the next time you are at home waiting for someone to return, and your dog suddenly goes on alert. Note the time, and how long it takes before the person actually arrives.

None of the three are shy about asserting themselves, though Killian, being twice Bear's size and probably three times Baby's, is a very gentle fellow who can take a lot of nagging and verbal abuse from the other two. Baby, particularly, likes to offer a very protective stance, especially when one of the others comes near her food bowl. That she lived free and wild for a while before she came to us through the SPCA, may explain her extraordinary aggressiveness in protecting her food, but no one gets near her bowl without having to swallow a pot full of growls and grumps. Killian, of course, tolerates this to the point that he even encourages it. Often, if things have been too quiet for too long, he will go and stand over her food dish as if he were about to swallow it whole, and maybe even nudge the edge once or twice. From wherever she is, Baby comes at full speed, growling and barking, only to find Killian sauntering off toward another room.

There was a time when Killian did the same thing with Bear. He would go in and pick up one of Bear's favorite toys, bring it into the room where the "little red dog" was lying, and very casually drop it, then pick it up, then drop it. When Bear would come barreling over to get it, Killi would drop it, and go to Bear's bowl and nudge it. Bear would then come running to his bowl, and the collie would go back and pick up the toy. Bear would come back to where the toy had been, Killi would drop it, go back to the food bowl, and they would repeat the cycle. As often as the big dog tried the trick, that's how often it worked.

Killian also has certain tasks he undertakes. For instance he helps make the bed. As the bedding gets pulled into place, he gets under it at the foot of the bed and lifts it up, then walks under it, back and forth until you tell him to stop. I think he figures that helps air the bed.

When I get up in the morning the dogs know it is time for walking. Usually, unless the weather is too miserable for me (rarely for them), as soon as I get dressed we leave the house, go down to the fields, and walk around them. It is about one-and-a-half miles, and we do it in about 30 minutes, which for me is a good pace. For the dogs it is slow enough for them to investigate every mouse nest, rabbit hole and groundhog den along the way, plus bathe in the river and occasionally run up the mountain after a phantom deer or bear. At the twenty minute mark we usually stop and I give out dog treats. They have to gather round and sit, and then they get their morsel. I then continue on, and they catch up and pass me. There is a gate between the two fields, and when I get there it is a signal to use up the rest of their stored energy. Killian and Bear indulge in a great, growling circular chase, during which Baby tries to get a snout in anywhere, but she is just too small. The other two go at it with bared fangs, snarling and growling and tussling until Bear throws Killian to the ground, his jaws holding tight on the big dog's ruff. Then it's up and chase again, as we progress up to the road. Once out of the fields, they know play-time is over, and they come straggling behind me until we reach the driveway leading up to the house. Then it's hell-for-leather up the drive and around the wood pile, finally coming to me as I reach the back garden where the rest of their treat is dispensed. Now these fast and furious creatures begin the slowest walk imaginable, up to the door and into the house, where they will suddenly collapse in their special places throughout the house, each a warm, panting, doggy-smelling heap. There they will lie until the next time a door is opened, or one of us walks to another room. Then it's up and on the move, following us from place to place, throwing themselves down, picking themselves up, again and again until they decide we aren't leaving or going to do something interesting.

Life with these dogs is a dance of which they never tire, and neither do we.

Walk Rabbit, Walk

Dogs, most owners will agree, are inveterate hunters. It is something that is part of their nature; a survival need going back to their wolfpack origins. Surely there is no more deeply rooted canine behavior than the response to scent and sight of another animal, regardless of size.

When Killian, Bear and Baby leave the house in the morning to walk around the fields, their progress is often interrupted by sniffing, nose thrusting, grass scratching and, occasionally, chasing. In the fields in front of the house, as well as in the gardens and mountainside around the house, rabbits are the most plentiful creatures on the ground. This year they certainly have out-bred the field mice and other bite-size mammals, and are so plentiful that one almost stumbles over them. Lately, however, the dogs seem to have lost their taste for the chase.

Several times recently, as we walked down the road, we've seen rabbits sitting alongside the roadway. They sit very still, bunched and ready to flee, but they wait until the last moment before diving into the underbrush. At first it seemed as though this was a purposeful act, designed to hide themselves by becoming invisible. Rabbits do that. So it seemed likely that the long eared hoppers were just relying on the dog's poor eyesight for their survival. But then it became more obvious what was going on. Especially the morning that Killian the Collie sauntered—sauntered, yes, not even a fast walk—sauntered up to this still-sitting bunny and, so it seemed from the resulting action, engaged in a discussion of how to proceed, especially since they were under observation. The result was that Rabbit got up and hopped away as the dog walked slowly behind him, stopping when he reached the brush at the edge of the road. As for the other dogs? Well, they just ignored the whole scene.

That wasn't the only exhibition witnessed on these walks. Usually it is just a simple example of a dog ignoring what is obviously too far away to make a good chase, or using what starts out as a chase as an excuse to divert into the river for a drink. Sometimes all three will begin a chase, streaming out in rank order (big, medium and little), diving into dense brush, then reappearing looking mystified, as though they had no idea where the quarry might have gone. It is obvious, though, that they gathered away from watchful eyes to catch up on what's been happening in the rabbit's life, how the kids are, that sort of thing.

Another time, Bear was at one end of the small field when he saw a rabbit about two thirds of the way up, along the edge. Going from canter to gallop, he went low to the ground, decreasing his wind resistance, and in short order was nearing the sitting target. The target, however, took two hops and was in the tall grass along the side. Bear never broke stride. Coming on at full speed, he ran past the still visible bunny. His head swiveled left, then returned to "eyes front," until he was some ten or twenty feet past the quarry. At which point he simply stopped running, looked at his master to see if his great run had been observed, and then walked on.

And if one needed more proof of the collusion among these "natural enemies," visualize this: we are walking, mostly together, around the end of the big field. There are several truckloads of wood chips, dumped there two years ago, surrounded by clumps of uncut hay and weeds. I lose sight of Killian the Collie as he goes around one of the piles, and begins sniffing at the back of it. Bear and Baby join him, then come around the pile to circle it slowly. Come around it—followed by a rabbit! Walk, rabbit, walk.

Doe Eyes

Hunting season began here about ten days ago, and finally the deer seem to be getting wind of what is up. Fewer than we were seeing even a week ago are making themselves visible during legal hunting hours. But during the last weeks of summer, and even into the first week of bow hunting, it was possible to see a dozen or so in the field across from the house, and three or four along the driveway.

Often, when I have been in the field with a tractor, mowing the last growth of the late season, I've come around a turn and found two or three grazing animals in an area I had just cut. They like having the work done for them, I think, because they seem to gravitate to the most recently cut areas. For some reason, the tractor doesn't scare them. If I am on foot, or if I stop to look at them, they will nervously continue eating until either the breeze changes and puts me upwind, or they just can't fight the anxiety any longer. Then one will snort, and the others will go on full alert, before bounding away into higher cover. But not always.

The other day I had been in the shed at the turn of the driveway, where I keep the tractors and the truck and other large equipment, and I was returning to the house when something caught my eye. It was a full-grown doe, and she was about 40 feet away, on the upper side of the driveway. I stopped and we looked at each other for a moment before she went back to eating what I suspect were mushrooms growing around an old oak stump. I tried not to look her in the eye, because it seems to me that if we don't make eye contact the encounters last longer. Slowly, looking away and then back at her, I advanced along the drive way. Walk a few feet, then stop. Look away, look over, look away. Walk again. Stop. With each advance, she would look up, then go back to pawing the ground, using her hoof to kick free what she wanted, then bending her neck and taking the tidbit with her lips. She moved, of course, but only to the next attraction. Finally I was within about 15 feet of the tree stump. Talking to her in a low, flat tone, I hoped to get closer, secretly wishing, I guess, that she would let me touch her, knowing that it wouldn't happen, but feeling that I wanted to reassure her that she was safe on my land. Trying, perhaps, to make up for the accidental death of one of her cohort a week earlier.

I had gone out with the dogs at about 7:45 for our usual morning circuit of the fields. As we came to the bottom of the driveway, two of the dogs suddenly raced to the edge of the road that divides our land into roughly two 60 acre parcels. On the east side the river cuts through, and deer come down the mountain behind the house to drink, and browse the fields. The dogs had seen or heard a deer trying to get away by going down the bank from the road, but unfortunately she had come up against a section of old fence that runs parallel to the road at the bottom of the bank. When I got to the edge, I saw that she had tried to go under the fence. Only her head and neck had made it, before the dogs were on her. Neither is big enough to cause serious harm, but still it took me a minute of harsh shouting to drive them away from her, and back onto the road. But now I had a dilemma of my own.

Being in close proximity to a live deer can be very dangerous. Their hooves can cut like knives, and their strength is not to be minimized. These are animals that can spring from a standing start over a six or seven foot fence. I suppose the position at the bottom of a bank, with the fence in front of her, led her to attempt to go under. It was not a loose enough opening, however, and she became trapped. The dogs kept her trying to go forward, when her only way out was to back up. She lay on her side, struggling to get under.

Having sent the dogs off, I positioned myself at her back, hoping that I could lift the fence enough for her to remove herself from the trap. Not thinking too hard about what would happen should she pull out and stand to face me, I worked at calming her and lifting the fence. When I had it up enough, I gently put my hand on her jaw and moved her head out. But it was already too late. In her panic, I think, she must have snapped her neck, because in a few minutes she stopped struggling, even though she was free, and gave up the fight. Her eyes rolled open and her breathing stopped. I felt very sad. We have far too many deer this year, and our garden and paths show the ravages of their appetite, so this one was really part of a problem, but still I hated to lose her this way. Hunting could at least provide food for someone's table. A death in total panic and fear though, would saturate the meat with adrenaline, and during such a warm spell as we have had, yield more parasites as well. I would not butcher her even if I was good at it.

Now, back on the driveway, the doe on the hillside and I continued to commune until, with a characteristic snort, she turned and headed back up the mountain. Not far, but enough for us to have a comfortable separation. I walked on, satisfied that she would remain wild, and that the course of her life would be guided by the predator/prey relationship, and that over time we might, just might, have the opportunity to get to know each other better.

Dependence, Independence, and Squirrels

I sit at my desk facing a window that looks out over a part of the deck that runs unbroken across most of the 120 feet of the South-facing front of the house. We used to keep bird feeders on poles at the edge of the deck where we could see them from the dining table, but about two years ago I moved them so we could see them from my office and my wife's studio.

Over the years I tried more schemes and ruses than I can remember to rid ourselves of the squirrels that ate the bird seed. There were feeders hung on wires that ran from tree to deck; feeders on poles with canopies half-way up between deck and feeder; slippery poles; arms from which the feeders hung, the arms encircled by over-size tubing that would roll with the squirrel's weight. And nothing much worked.

When you have trees that overhang the deck, railings that line it, and squirrels that are acrobats, you just don't succeed. You either give up, give in, or stop feeding the birds if the squirrels annoy you enough. Or you find a solution.

When we moved the feeders we also replaced them with a kind that includes a long clear plastic cylinder, a metal top that slides up and down on the wire bail or handle, and at the bottom, a circular perch that, when the weight is right, is spun by an electric motor. The weight is anything from a blue jay plus one or two nuthatches to a squirrel. The feeders hang from arms that angle up and outward from the deck railing. From our windows we can watch the finches, cardinals, nuthatches, and other small birds fill on sunflower seeds. And we can watch the squirrels become frustrated.

Now, it's not that the squirrels have no other source of food. Our land abounds in pines, oaks, hickory and walnut trees, lots of green shoots on the ground, and (not to be shunned) sunflower seeds on the ground knocked down by the birds on the feeders. They don't starve. They are fat. They have gotten fat by doing what they are programmed to do: eat where nature, not we, place the food.

But back to learning. In the years we had the feeders on poles and hung from wires and trees, the squirrels could figure out how and where to launch an attack that was almost always successful. From a branch above, a clever one could drop right on top of the feeder, bend over and gorge. Or from a branch, reach the horizontal wire, walk out to where the feeder hung, slide down and sit on the feeder. From the ground it was a calculation of angles and lift worthy of NASA to leap to the feeder, pull itself up, and take over the station. Anti-gravity? These guys knew the answer eons ago. So what happened when we put the new feeders up?

The squirrels come daily in the Fall. They walk along the railing of the deck, climb easily up the slanted arm to the hook where the feeder hangs, and then step onto the top of the feeder. Then they try to lift the top, but they are sitting on it. Not a possible solution. Then they will hold on with their hind feet and stretch down to reach the feeder ports, but they just aren't long enough. So they give up. Go away. Turn around and come back and repeat the whole act again, maybe two or three times before they give up. Until the next time. But if they can jump from the ground to the feeder, why can't they jump from the deck to the feeder that hangs out a mere three feet? The answer is obvious: they have learned that if they grab on the perch they get a free ride, but no food. It has happened once or twice that we've witnessed, but that was the first year we put these feeders out. And those squirrels seemed to do it by stretching from the top down until they were able to reach the perch, then swing down. Of course they were then flung out and off, hitting the ground surprised but unharmed. Are the current attempts being made by shorter squirrels? Perhaps those too young to have been part of the first year's cohort? Or have the tricks of these new feeders now been imprinted in the group memory? I don't know.

I'm happy to see them make decisions based on what's best not just for themselves, but for the birds, too. And for us. Where we used to use fifty pounds of black oil sunflower seed in as little as a week, we now feed the birds for a month or more. And with the cost of seed going up (remember, it has "oil" in the name), that's welcome too. But the best part is that we see the small birds feeding regularly, we still get a beautiful show of animal agility, and we know we are a friendly place for all to visit. Friendly but challenging.

Is there a lesson here for us all? I think so. It's not a question of a free lunch: the antics of the squirrels, the harmony of the birds, more than repay our investment, and extract a sound payment from the animals. It is what life should offer, and what we should demand in our own lives: pay for what you get, provide something in return, and never, never give up.

Part V—Baggage Car

The Man I Used To Be

"Things ain't what they used to be and probably never was."—Will Rogers

I'm not the man I used to be. When I was a very young man, more than half-a-century ago, I was bright, dynamic, creative, forceful, cynical, acerbic, witty, humorous, tall, dark, and handsome. I was a formidable package!

In conversation I was known for being quick with a biting observation or retort. I was able to regale listeners with oddly skewed versions of events, or outrageous points of view about most everything.

As a writer I could grasp a situation or series of events and convert that into film scripts of powerful images, narration and dialogue. If a given scene was of a specific length, I could write, without planning, the exact number of words necessary to fill the time. As the words poured out they keyed to specific shots without my consciously trying. I was known for fast response, excellent rhythm, and poor typing and even worse spelling.

With women I was a master: kind, considerate, aloof, reserved, "interesting," and hard to catch. When I was "caught," I was in control, able to direct the relationship and, when it was over, I was able to walk away, ignoring the rubble, to seek another.

To employers, colleagues and friends alike I was known as a man who could be depended upon; who took his work, but very little else, seriously; who stood by his commitments and obligations (if I were so unwise as to incur any).

But was I all of that?

In this new world of perpetual youth, I am older, getting older, aging, and (dare I suggest) wiser. I can look back with some objectivity and amusement at what "callow youth" really means, examine the egocentric image of a boy-man, replay scenes of memory and dreams. Where in all of that is the man I used to be? Where, behind the hands that type these words, is the Lascaux Cave that holds those images I illuminate with a torch of memory? Do the paintings on the walls of my mind really represent the world I inhabited, or are they mere smudges that have been left by the fire that burned and still illuminates? Do we all see so tinted a vision of our past?

When I was born the world was still in the grip of the Great Depression. There had been other times as bad, of course, and times to come even worse in terms of human suffering and the dislocation of lives. But by the 1930's the world had arrived at the stepping-off place leading to global communications; a world so new and beckoning that few perceived the potential for (as in all things) good and evil. What happened to all of us happened to each of us, but so had it always been. The difference now was that perception, not judgement, began to overwrite understanding. Thus what could have been an economic setback turned, because of the speed of communication, into a global disaster. Judgement, calm reason, factual analysis all went out the window as quickly as bodies on Wall Street. (Another perception: the actual number of broken fortunes that converted to broken bodies was far smaller than the image generally presented of that time.) Panic, an emotional response to deep-rooted fear, led to one tumble after another; one more trip on the down staircase.

When my father was born, on the fourth day of the new century, more people walked than rode, could talk than could write, listen than read. All looked up at the moon. None looked down from it. By the time I was born, at just about the halfway point in his life, the world moved on powered wheels, and powered wings, and communicated by wire and wireless. By the time his life was over, the moon was a launching pad, and the universe was a neighborhood. We could see farther, but were we what we could see? Were we all image?

Somewhere, between the world into which I was born, and the world in which I now live, the boy grew into a man, lived a productive and interesting life, and now has time to look back and reflect on what sort of man I was and am. I know now that there were times when, in spite of my self confidence and self control, I was scared, unsure, even fearful of the world. Not all of it, and often not in the places where perhaps I should have been, but those emotions folded themselves around me, cinching my waist, squeezing my shoulders, darkening my world. Yet I managed to overcome those emotions and get on, pursuing goals, attaining acceptance, acknowledging defeat, redirecting and surmounting the daily twists and turns life brings.

I used my ability to see the world in my own way to find philosophies that have sustained and nurtured me, strengthened and empowered me. One is that there is nothing in the universe that someone before me hasn't already had to overcome, and except for the ultimate experience, if they have overcome it, so might I. Another is that if you have all your fingers and toes, then you get out of life exactly what you want…whether you know it or not. I've had my doubts, of course, my failures and unsatisfying successes, too. But when I examine the challenges I have faced, look at the places I have been, recall the fortune in love and laughter that has been mine, I believe that my philosophies have served me well.

Still, I am the man I came to be. I'm not the man I used to be, and I probably never was.

On Understanding Sacrifice

This essay dates from 2000. At the time my mother, well into her 90s, still lived alone in the house where my sister and I did most of our growing up. It was a place where we learned many of the lessons that have brought us to where we are today.

I was visiting my mother a few weeks ago, and as usual, I spent some of the time fixing a few things around the house. I needed a hammer and a nail, so I went to the drawer in her kitchen where for at least the last 50 years a collection of odd tools and other hardware could always be found.

As I rummaged through the contents, I turned up an electric soldering iron, c. 1948. About 12 inches long, with a barrel about half-an-inch in diameter, and a red wooden handle, I recognized the iron as one of the first "real" tools I had purchased. Just touching the metal I instantly recalled the first night I had it, and how, in the process of getting acquainted with its properties, I had grabbed it around the barrel between my thumb, index and middle fingers. I felt again the searing pain, and in milliseconds of recall I realized I could still feel the exact points of contact as if I had just gripped the iron. As I looked at it I remembered hiding from my parent the fact that I had burned myself. In the night the pain became intense and I remember grasping the cold metal bed spring to bring some relief. I recalled, too, the really stupid feeling I had of doing something that dumb. But it shouldn't have surprised me: I had been (and still am) doing those kinds of things throughout my life with tools.

MIXED FREIGHT

One of my earliest and most vivid memories has to do with plunging a pair of rusty garden scissors into the web between thumb and index finger of my left hand. I couldn't have been more than three, but I can still see me, the screened porch where it happened, the wide, flat, pointed brown blades. There is still a scar to remind me of that moment.

And so it has gone from that time forth. I suppose I could simply accept the fact that I am dangerous to myself (implement challenged), but the fact is that I rather look on those incidents and the hundreds and hundreds of other cuts and abrasions as simply sacrifices, perhaps to Thor; sacrifices demanded of those who work with their hands. I almost feel unfulfilled if I accomplish a job without the loss of at least a microsliver of skin. Over the years working with tools, doing everything from model airplanes to house building, toy repair to auto mechanics, I must have pinched or cut or scraped sufficient skin to build at least a whole hand, maybe more. And it isn't that I don't realize the risks. Even the time I nipped off an eighth of an inch of fingertip on a jointer, I saw the potential, and even heard in my head the words, "this could be very dangerous." Except that the fingertip was entering the last interstice between the spinning blades, even as I recognized the thought. The job was ultimately completed very satisfactorily, so the sacrifice must have been acceptable, and certainly the damage could have been much more severe.

Looking at my hands as I write this, I count a barked knuckle given while installing some shelves in my wife's studio and a cut on my thumb offered while trimming a piece of plastic supply tubing for a new faucet.

And did I find the hammer? Yes, two in fact: a worn but serviceable claw hammer with a steel handle, and a ball peen. Like the ones in my own tool boxes, it must have come from one of my father's automobile tool kits of the kind not supplied in probably more than half-a-century. And the sacrifice? Well, all I was going to do was reset a finishing nail in a bannister rail. Going up the stairs to do the job, running my hand along the railing, as I took the last step, the side of my finger caught the slightly raised head of the nail.

    The bannister, need I add, is again solidly mounted.

Mr. Inbetween

I don't exactly put things off. More, it's that I put things aside. It is a matter of doing something now while waiting for another thing to happen later. It is a mode of life that was well suited to the work I did for so many years.

From my school days on I began compartmentalizing and putting things "on hold" (though that term hadn't yet gained the currency it subsequently has). It was a way of dealing with things happening out of sequence, as it were. We all experience it: you start something, then discover you need a piece of material or information that you don't have. While you are waiting for it to arrive, or to go and get it, you begin something else. Then that stalls, but if you are lucky the part you originally were looking for shows up and you go back to project number one. Or start number three. Soon you find you have a whole shelf of unfinished things, some of which linger on for years, while others die a quick death from neglect or just lack of interest or time.

If you have lived from deadline to deadline as I did for so many years, if you spent as much time with the military, then you know how it goes. Hurry up and wait is the usual coda. Sometimes, however, it is more than you can stand, and you just grab everything on the desk or workbench or truck bed and dump it. I developed a six-month rule when I was working full-time: incoming work went into a tray. If it didn't surface in six months it went into the trash. In my workshop at home there were similar project piles; some craft or repair started but unfinished for lack of a part or a tool or a can of something.

They have had a longer life span, I think because I felt that my time was so fractioned that six months could span a few years. Then there are these essays and at least three books in draft form. One short story I finished in 1999 was first drafted in 1959, based on a incident I witnessed in 1956! Whatever it is that happens, it isn't chronometric.

The point is that we seem to spend so much of our lives waiting for things to coincide, to erupt, to just happen, and in the meantime we go on doing other things, important and trivial, that make up the bulk of our lives. Well, I for one am not yet ready to change. It is comfortable, it is sometimes productive, and most of all, it keeps me from feeling that I am rushing to conclusion. Plenty of time for that, don't you agree?

Since this was written (2001), one novel, Accidents of Time and Place, (PublishAmerica, 2007) and these essays have found their way into print. The other novels are still "in writing."

Woodworker's Wood

For as long as I can remember, working with wood has been a hobby and a passion. I have carved, cut, turned and assembled all kinds of wooden things, from simple "whatzits" to whole buildings. Over the years I have learned to cut, join, sand and finish many kinds of wood, and in the process I have acquired some knowledge of the characteristics of different species and grades of this most workable of natural materials.

Some of the knowledge has come slowly and painfully. Cuts, splinters, bruises, falls have all been part of the learning process, and while I can't say that I have truly mastered any of the skills, I am capable of taking a project from idea to completion, and the end result serves.

A little of what I have learned has come relatively painlessly, and much still eludes me. For instance, I first learned about wood from the end product. Furniture, observed from the floor up, which is the way most babies and children first confront it, teaches some early lessons about what is good to bump, and what is easy to upset and move. Wood can be heavy or light, soft or hard, dark or light, dull or shiny, taste sweet or sharp or bitter. In many ways wood can be a metaphor for life.

Early on I learned to recognize pine by its smell and soft, white/yellow color. Oak was something solid and heavy, mahogany deep purple, and maple had a peculiar smell. As time went on I began to recognize grain patterns and knot figures, presence or lack of splinters, and other traits you learn only from handling wood as a material.

My earliest recollection of wood is from a period when I was perhaps five or six, and my parents were having some work done to finish off the attic in our one-story house. The carpenter came every day, and every evening I would go up and gather all the little scraps, usually triangles cut from studs being installed to frame out what is known as a "knee wall" (I suppose because it is only knee-high). I can still recall the smell of the pitchy, rough edges, and the sticky feeling if a little got on my hands. I would use the bits to stack up imaginary buildings and fortresses, add wheels from old toys, or empty sewing thread spools, to make primitive carts and cars, or find animal shapes in the trimmed ends to fill out a circus wagon I had built.

In school, after having played with wood for years, I finally took "shop." That was probably the most looked-forward-to class I ever had after I learned to read, and I can't think of another since that has given me such life-long resources and pleasure. I had my first exposure to real tools, beyond the old hand saw, rusty hammer and other homeowner necessities my father had around. I learned about power tools and fine wood working tools, lathe and drill press, plane and chisel and even glue and clamp techniques. What I didn't learn was about the source of the material I used.

As a boy I often spent time in the woods near our home. These were usually solo walks just to enjoy being outside. I loved the smells of the woods, and sounds of the birds and ground scurrying animals, the way light worked down between the leaves and branches. Even today I enjoy just looking up through the branches of trees to see the changing pattern of light as the sun moves across the sky. But for some reason, I never thought to try to identify what trees I saw.

I knew a pine, of course. In Piedmont North Carolina pines are as common as red dirt. And eventually I came to know the difference between an oak leaf and a maple leaf. The individual trees, however, escaped my grasp. Not so in the shop. Pine cuts easily, cedar is a "hard" soft wood, oak can bend a nail, and maple can take the teeth off a saw; hardly a tree lover's guide to identification, but for the woodworker, it works.

I have also learned about species as a woodcutter. For years we have heated our homes with wood, cutting it on our property in Virginia, hauling it to the Maryland suburb where we lived, and splitting and stacking it and burning it. Nothing teaches you about the character of wood like taking a tree down, cutting it into moveable pieces, hauling, splitting, stacking and burning. You quickly identify those trees that will cut safely, which ones will take the edge off a new chain fastest, and what kind of force is needed to split a particular kind of round with a maul. As for hauling and stacking, you can learn a lot about wood from lifting it. Things like how much heat you can expect from how much effort. Btu's are not the only measure of heat output!

But still, I hadn't really begun to identify trees by name until we moved permanently from Maryland to our land here on Virginia's Northwestern frontier. Living on the edge of the Allegheny chain, our trees run the gamut from white pine to sugar maple. We have white oak and red oak and several other sub-species, as well as sycamore, chestnut, walnut, hickory and locust. There are patches of a wood called hornbeam, and growths of thin trunks known hereabouts as "trash trees." I'm pretty conversant with the names because I have had the timber "cruised" prior to some cutting, and the report identifies most of the species we have, and where on our original 380 acres they are found. I have only to look at the reports and know what I have. Little by little, as I walk my fields and woods, I am coming to know the trees when I see them "dressed" with their bark on, and sometimes even with their leaves off.

The only disturbing factor in all of this is the presence of "fakewood," as opposed to what one furniture manufacturer I know calls "realwood." Included in this are veneers on manufactured substrate made from woodchips, or even recycled plastics and paper. Even more difficult are the better plastic finishes that look like wood but aren't even attached to it. It may serve to provide a tough, work-a-day surface, but it will never have the feel or smell (or taste) of the real thing. It reminds me of a term I first heard from a friend when we were in high school. His father was a furrier, who worked with things like "mink-dyed rabbit" and other hyphenated materials. Today we have "oak-grained" plastics that look like the real thing (if you aren't too close), but have about the same value over time as the rabbit in mink's coloring.

I wonder what I would have learned about wood if, when I was just learning about the world, everything had been something that looked like something else. Perhaps I would have become a politician.

Finderman

I've always had a habit of looking down when I walk, keeping my eyes on the ground. When I was a student I walked to school almost everyday; a few blocks to elementary school, to junior high about two miles south, and to high school about two miles north of our home. Over the years I added pens, mechanical pencils, or odd bits of jewelry (none valuable) to my pockets as I walked. Coins—pennies and dimes, mostly—were another product of my ground search.

Along with my ability to find things I developed a visual sense that allowed me to recall the surroundings of seen objects; very useful when putting something down and then going back to get it. If I couldn't immediately locate something, I could stop, visualize the motions and surroundings related to putting the thing down, and go unerringly to it.

As I have grown older, I have retained the finding skills, but I have developed some losing skills as well. I can't always recall the scene, for instance, when I am looking for something I have put down. It is most frustrating, especially when it is, say, a small part or a screw or nut and bolt I have just removed from something I am working on, and I'm ready to reinstall it. Then I sort of rely on a process that begins with trying to sense the object. I can "feel" it calling to me, but I think along with other aging processes, my hearing has also lost some of its keenness.

So I have developed a more systematic method of searching. If I drop something on the floor, for instance, especially something small, I will tell myself that I have one chance to recover it. That helps me focus on the object, and I will usually see it. It is true, though, that if I drop it again, it is probably lost forever—or at the very least until I have made a substitution.

Going beyond things I have lost immediately before I begin looking for them, the dropped part or the mis-placed screw, I have found great success by applying the following colloquy: "Where is the place it is most unlikely to be? If it is where it should be, then I would have found it, so it must be where it is not supposed to be." A pair of glasses, for instance, which should be on a desk, will invariably show up at the other end of the house. The checkbook, last seen in the kitchen, will be under the seat of the car. Gloves, shoes, all the mobile things in our lives, will eventually show up; remember that matter cannot be destroyed or created, but can only change. Ergo, as the scientists say, the object is not lost, it has simply changed environments. Q.E.D., look where it isn't supposed to be.

So successful is this method that I am often called upon to retrieve another's missing eyeglasses, or checkbook or keys or other wandering property. I look where things aren't supposed to be, or where logic says it can't be. Sometimes the loser is absolutely positive it was last seen in a certain place, and that it isn't there any longer, so I will immediately look under or over or even in the place identified as where the object was "last seen." Sometimes I can find it where the owner has looked just before I came on the search, only a layer down, or a foot to the side.

We expect things to be where we remember them being, rather like our youth, but too often it is something we must seek elsewhere. Around our house it becomes "Another job for FINDERMAN!"

Fear and the Thrill of Meeting the Challenge

"You gain strength, courage and confidence by every experience in which you really stop to look fear in the face...I say to myself, I've lived through this and can take the next thing that comes along...We must do the things we think we cannot do."—Eleanor Roosevelt

I was raised to be afraid. For my parents, perhaps it was the shock of having taken risks in the twenties, followed by the losses of the thirties that left them with a distrust of risk, or perhaps it was simply the make-up of their personalities. Coming from immigrant backgrounds, both were faced with varying degrees of effort to make a life in a new world.

My father had the easier of the two lives. His father and grandfather had come to Philadelphia (where my father was born), and then to New York City, where they successfully pursued real estate and investing as a way of life, neither of which, I think, are without risk. In 1917, my grandfather moved his family (my father and his three brothers) to North Carolina to establish a new business venture. For a European and a Jew to leave the international environment of a place like New York for the rather homogenous South was itself a remarkable display of risk-taking.

My mother, on the other hand, was an itinerant's daughter. He was a shop-keeper who had no head for business, nor any real desire to own a store. He was a peddler for a while, a soldier, a farmer who couldn't make a go of that, either, but who wanted to give his family a better life than Russia and the Czar offered. Still, his children survived, my mother to immigrate with her mother after grandfather had established" himself; the others to be born here. I don't know how he measured success, because by any contemporary standards he was probably a failure. His daughter loved him, and respected him, and wanted to emulate his devotion to God and to scholarship, so I would have to say that in the things that really mattered, he was a success. He was also a man who took risks, leaving the Czar's army after the Russo-Japanese War, traveling to Argentina to become part of a back-to-the land movement led by Theodore Herzl, then returning to Russia before immigrating to America where he, too, settled in a very small Southern town. He soon sent for his wife and daughter (my mother), and began building his shop-keeper's life.

When I was growing up I was always cautioned, always being told about limits, about being hurt or getting sick or some other consequence of stepping out of the ordinary. Climbing a tree, riding a tricycle, going down hill on a borrowed Flexie (the Southern version, I guess, of the Flexible Flyer sled—it was equipped with wheels). Sometimes those activities did lead to pain, to bandages and even to the discomfort of having my ribs encased in adhesive plaster for several weeks one summer. Still I kept on trying new things, at least until I reached an age where fear was more palpable. Then, for a long time, I distanced myself from exposure, walked away from challenges, found reasons to not try or act. I was afraid. Somewhere along the way, a time or place or situation I cannot remember, I took a risk or two, and didn't suffer for it. Instead, I felt a surge of power, a thrill that nothing before had generated within me.

Did that influence my life? Of course. As I look back, almost everything, choice of career, marriage, even retirement have

MIXED FREIGHT

had elements of risk the ordinary person would turn away from, or at least think of as a burden. For me it was always a challenge. Sometimes I would have to hold myself, like a swimmer holding his nose as he jumps feet-first into the deep pool of the river. There is something about stepping off into the unknown, carrying, in my case, a full load of fear, that when it is over, the jump accomplished, there comes a feeling of growth and success that is unlike anything else. I cannot describe it, I cannot duplicate it. It is something that must be experienced to understand.

As I look back, I see two things, two different philosophies that have guided my life; have made me the man I have become. One, and by far the more unusual I think, is that I early on learned to profit from another's experience. It became a part of my innermost response process to listen and avoid those actions and behavior patterns which might have been costly to me. My first model for this was my older sister. I saw and remembered the acts and responses that brought on parental wrath, and avoided duplicating her mistakes. Later on, as I found my way in the world, I tended to pass by opportunities that might have been rewarding, but offered a high degree of risk. By and large I have found it to be a sound policy. If I didn't always profit from it, I at least avoided some pain. Some, but not all. That has been the other guiding principle.

In time, though, I learned to face fear, to challenge it, to look beyond it. When faced with something difficult, an act fraught with danger or demanding extreme (for me) physical effort, or even just something totally beyond my experience and understanding, I have said to myself: "This is not something new which no man has ever done. What I am being called upon to do is not being done for the first time. If someone else has done it and survived, then chances are I can, too." And when each challenge has been met, I have felt a surge of confidence and reward unlike any other sensation. I have taken the stick in a small plane, driven race cars in competition, been where war is, walked down dark streets in modern cities. I have worked as a freelance in a competitive business, been responsible for the employment of others, stood up and made speeches off the cuff in public meetings. I am ready to meet the final challenge when it comes. I am no longer afraid of life, or living, or dying.

In a Word, Yes

Much, if not all, of the success I have had in life, I owe to the word "yes." I'm not sure where I learned it, probably from my father. He was a salesman who was "on the road" for 55 years, and he built his success on a reputation for satisfying his customers, even if it meant going beyond showing a product and writing an order. Whatever the customer asked for, if his company could supply it or find it, he would, I know, say "yes." It is a word that has worked well for me, too.

In my professional life, responding to the needs of clients with many different objectives, I early on developed the habit of simply saying "yes" to any request for services. My staff, when I had one, learned to expect that I would approve any project, regardless of what was involved. I would say "yes," they knew, and worry about the "how" and "when" later.

At some point, years before I retired, I began saying "yes" when asked to volunteer, usually in some professional organization. It is another habit I still have, and still find myself over committed (alas, not in my own mind until it becomes stressful), still saying "yes."

I suppose such an approach is evidence of a supreme confidence in other people, as well as in myself. I always have succeeded at the task before me, even though at the beginning I might not be able to visualize what the end might be. And I have always had confidence in the people I have had working with me. When I hired a new employee I looked for one who knew more than I, or had fresher ideas. And always, I looked for the attitude that would produce the word I needed to hear: "yes."

Yes we can, regardless of what the "can" may hold. Yes we will, regardless of the way ahead. Yes, because if you begin looking for the reasons not to, you will find them all around you: other people's failures, imploded or crashed initiatives and inventions, immolated dreams.

Saying "yes" before you think about what you will need to do to accomplish the task thrusts you forward to success.

I suppose in a way saying "yes" is a response from the part of me that likes to be accepted, recognized as an individual. It is also a confirmation that I am part of the thrilling and rewarding struggle to improve myself and my world.

In my early years, writing scripts for documentary and educational films, I would worry about where the words would come from, where the ideas for structure and image would be found. It took a long time, and a lot of "yes," to realize that I didn't need to know the source. I had only to remember that it was there when I needed it. It required only a commitment to "yes."

For a long time now, I have not given much thought to how, or where, or when I would accomplish something promised. If a proposal or a challenge excites my imagination, I know it will be accomplished; that all it takes is a word from me. Success is, in a word, "yes."

Living Treasure

I have begun an inventory of the several collections I have built over the years. Books, old pieces of machinery and antique tools, a number of stick pins (most from the Victorian age when men wore them in their cravats), old watches and a clock or two, and antique cameras are just some of the things I have acquired over a lifetime. I've decided to start getting rid of all or most of what I have.

This isn't a sudden whim. It has been on my mind for some time. I am getting to the point where possessions weigh more heavily than they did. About a year ago, following an unexpected confrontation with getting older, I began thinking that the time had come to simplify my life, and to make some preparation for the future. Now these "things" seem more burdensome than pleasurable. They are something to conserve, be concerned about protecting, establishing and maintaining some mechanism just to have them available to look at.

Most of us who treasure treasures (for that is what these things are) too often hold on to them physically long after we have made them our own intrinsically, leaving it for the heirs to dispose. Usually that results in a loved collection being broken up and reduced in value. So now I am thinking about getting rid of some of these things. I don't even want to contemplate their ending up on some yard sale table (25¢ hardbound, 10¢ paperback) or trucked off to the thrift shop. Not because of the money—that doesn't matter—but because all of these things were collected for their own sake. They have a beauty, a soul-swelling, pulse-elevating quality that has enhanced the world for all who require a gracious and soft-edge compartment in their daily lives.

We both collect books, art, and *tshatshkes*. The books are in the library, some of them read over and over, but it is the mere sight of them, the smell of old pages and ideas with real substance that make them valuable to us. The art hangs on the walls and adds measurably to our world. But the collection of antique tools, old hardware and machinery bits are under the work bench in my shop, or in boxes in a storage building. Car parts and automobiliana are in boxes in the garage and one of the sheds. They appeal to me, but I have no room to spread them out, no wall space to display them. Yet when I uncover them, looking for something else, I stop to enjoy them again, to touch and take from them some richness of, and contact with, another time; of a master hand that wanted to fulfill an artist's destiny. In another, less expansive time, every worker who made something for use was an artisan—part artist, part craftsman—who transmitted a little beauty to those who used the finished product. A tool, a piece of furniture, a garment, each had an element of creativity incised on, or woven into it.

Who will want them when I'm gone, or when I am too old to even remember where they are? Like everything else, there is a season…besides, I recently acquired an antique tractor I plan to restore, and I really need room for the second one I am buying for parts.

Time Marches On

It began with a clock. One of my earliest memories—I was perhaps three or so—is sitting on the floor demolishing a broken alarm clock. I wasn't doing it out of rage, but out of curiosity. I wanted to know "what made it tick." It is a trait which has never left me. Even today, when I remove a broken or failed part from an appliance, I will reduce it to its components just to see what's inside, what makes it tick.

My fascination with things mechanical probably began with my first baby rattle, and has grown in both sophistication and size as I have grown up and older. Machines, machinery and the technology that they embody have held my attention, attracted my curiosity, even been responsible for some painful lessons regarding the placement of fingers and energizing of muscles.

Cuts, sprains, just plain pain have been intermixed with the satisfaction of acquiring knowledge, of repairing something otherwise useless, making an object do a job for which it wasn't originally designed; a kind of "Yankee ingenuity." It is, I think, an American trait that has served this nation well. It is the source of Edison's genius, of Ford's creativity, of the many thousands of inventors and inventions that have defined our nation. In my own small way, I have been a part of that tradition: the shade-tree mechanic, the tinkerer, the "Mr. Fixit" for my family and friends for as long as I can remember.

As my world expanded from rattles to more formed toys, I began to look at cars, trucks and other kinds of powered devices with great fascination. Over the years, from the age of about 15, I have acquired, worked on, been frustrated by, beggared by and enthralled by more than 30 cars, trucks, and just recently, a tractor. Another image in my mind is a small red tractor, perhaps a replica of a Farmall, that occupied my play time nearly three-quarters of a century ago. To own a real one, of any make, has been at the back of my mind for a long time. I think what has always attracted me is the idea that this is a machine that has a genuine purpose, is devoid of any frills and unnecessary parts such as doors, fenders, and the like, and can do a job a man cannot do easily or well alone. It is a machine with a reason for being. There is a whole philosophy bound up in those thoughts, I guess: that technological advancement is that which allows the hand of man to be multiplied, or strengthened, or simply extended to accomplish something necessary. "A man's reach must exceed his grasp." In the pursuit of machines, and the tools with which they are made and repaired, I have seen the decline of respect for work march in lock-step with the decline in beauty of the tools we used to use. Functional design has replaced art in the creation and construction of machinery, and along with that, I believe, respect for the work we do with our hands, and the genuine usefulness of that labor.

Look at a hand saw, for example. About twenty to thirty inches long, of a particular shape and texture, it has a row of finely ground teeth, each very sharp and set at a precise angle to the face of the blade. Once that was a job, just keeping the "set" and sharpness of a blade. If you have an old one in your shop, you will immediately notice two things: first, the handle is of wood, not plastic, and it is decorated with flutes and swirls, and assembled with brass fittings, in what I like to think is a salute to the craftsman who first used it. It was not enough to make a tool that worked; it also must have some beauty, something that at once inspired and pleased the user. Tools and machines from an earlier time, say from the beginning of the industrial revolution to about the 1920's are all marked by this sense of art, as in artisan, or one who works at a skilled trade. These embellishments didn't try to obscure the function of the tool, but instead helped give sense and meaning to the user. So it is with a tractor. It is a prime mover, a powerful extension, a worker to do one's bidding.

My particular toy is about ten years younger than I, and still working. It will, at some point, be fully restored to its original state, but even then it will continue to help me in tasks I can not easily do otherwise, such as mowing big fields. Part of its charm is the purposefulness of its design, the open engine compartment, the lack of fenders and windshield. It is the essence of itself, as well as the tool it presents itself to be. There is no mistaking what it is, and what it will do. Each time I use it I learn something more about it, and I understand anew how necessary machines have been to the development and success of our nation. That doesn't make this any less a toy, or any more a milestone, but it does represent my own interests in several ways.

First, of course, it is useful, so I can justify the investment in both time and money. Tools, unlike toys, are meant to work and that dovetails with my own rather puritanical side which rejects pleasure just for pleasure. Not always, and not in everything, but as a general rule.

That first tractor was a 1946 Ford 2N. Eventually, after working on it and with it for several years I decided it wasn't needed. How wrong I was! Every farm, even one that grows only rocks and trees, needs a tractor. In 2009 I acquired a 60 year-old Farmall that alternately gets used and restored. Some toys you never outgrow.

Sleeping In Chairs

I come from a tradition of chair sleeping. It serves me well. If the chair is the right size, I can sleep in it. Time of day, environment, activity surrounding the chair—none of that matters. Just be a chair, and I can sleep in it.

When I was young I knew who my father was. In a photograph made about 1912, my father sits surrounded by his three brothers. By the time I was nine or ten, strangers visiting our home would look at the picture and ask me, "Where are your bothers?" So much alike were my father and I that I used to say I was never bothered by the usual childhood fantasy of being adopted; that these couldn't be my parents. That, I have always felt, gives a young man a certain sense of self and place, this knowing so incontrovertibly who your father is.

My father died when he was 72, and I was 37. Not too many years after his death I began to have "encounters." I would see a reflection in a mirror or window, and recognize him/see me looking back. Something funny would happen and I would hear him/me chuckle. Now in my sixties, I have come to recognize that chuckle as a sign that something had/has touched him/me at an emotional level. Not enough to bring tears, but almost.

Even in my twenties, people I didn't know, or hadn't seen in years would say, "You sure look like Al." Once, on a business trip back to my home state, I registered at a small hotel, and the first thing the desk clerk said, after looking at my card, was, "You must be Al's boy." My father, a traveling salesman for more than half a century, stayed in that hotel probably once a month, for who knows how many years.

So it should not disturb me that, now in my later years, I find myself sleeping in chairs. That's what my father did.

He was no lay-about, my father. He began working a man's work in his teens, and never stopped. The Saturday he died could have been the end of any week in the previous 55 years. He finished a full week of travel on Friday night, just as he had done nearly every week in any of those years. And I'm sure that the night before, after dinner, after synagogue, he sat in his big chair in the living room and slept. It was often a subject of derision for our mother, but as kids my sister and I thought it the most normal (and least contentious) of his habits.

But now I sleep in chairs. Especially (but not exclusively) after dinner. Part of it has to do with finding it difficult to sit still for any length of time, except by locking myself into a position of comfort, and letting my body slow down. I long ago gave up still hunting, because sitting quietly waiting for a deer to come near was either excruciatingly painful, or sleep inducing. Either condition would preclude "getting" (as opposed to hunting), because I would either squirm around or fall asleep.

And sleeping in a chair has become a sort of answer when I can't sleep. I go to bed but sleep won't come; I fall asleep and my twitching and snoring awakens my wife to the point of waking me; if I come home at three or four in the morning from an emergency call, so tired I can hardly keep awake on the drive from rescue squad building to garage, going to bed is no answer. I will still lie awake for another hour or two. And if my wife is away, well I might as well not even bother to turn back the bed. For as many nights as she is away, or if I am away myself, being in bed is antithetical to sleep.

But a chair! Just let me sit comfortably, or even rigidly, in a chair, and I'm asleep in minutes. I will sleep through the night, for the same four or five hours I can sleep soundly in bed (when I can), and awake refreshed and ready for the day.

Sleeping in chairs? Yes, and so was my old man!

Have a Piece Fruit

One of my least fond memories of childhood is of accompanying my parents on visits to relatives. It would almost always mean a day indoors. Indoors in the summer for a kid especially, is a day lost. Indoors in the home of a relative, or an elderly, perhaps sick friend, is not the same as being in your own home. There, at least you can go in or out in familiar surroundings.

Mostly I remember fruit. In those days, in my family, fruit—especially out-of-season fruit—was a thing to covet and hoard. In the last years of the depression and the war years that followed, fruit was as much a treat as candy.

The rooms were always dark and perfumed with tobacco smoke. At least some of the women were cigarette smokers. My father, his brothers and most of the other men, were cigar smokers and in my olfactory memory I could, for years, recapture glimpses of those visits, triggered by the smell of tobacco and fresh fruit. Apples, peaches, and bananas are the scents I remember most vividly. At least the fruit gave me something to look forward to.

Children in those days were oohed and ahhed over, then expected to fade away and be quiet. I recall very few visits to relatives with children until after the war, and they were either much too young to be interesting or so much older that we inhabited different worlds. If there were no other children, there was little to do. One sat and tried to look interested and hoped someone would pass the fruit bowl, and perhaps a dish of hard candy. If the visit was to a relative or family friend in a strange city, going outside alone was just not done.

Do people still visit relatives? Are those visits still conducted indoors in quiet dark rooms? Most of our visits were during the summer in years when houses were not air-conditioned and inside temperatures were moderated only by keeping the rooms dark, and by fans that often obscured conversation. Sometimes the temperatures made it too hot even for a little kid to be running around. So we sat, and we ate fruit and we learned about our families and their friends. And when it was time to go an uncle would quietly but ostentatiously slip a dollar into your pocket, pat you on the head and say: "You've been a good boy, I hope to see you soon again."

All of this, because I'm now at the age where we visit friends and relatives who are older, and again I find myself in rooms kept dim or dark and the only thing missing is the child I was. All the rest remains the same. Have a piece of fruit.

If I Knew What I Was Doing

Sunday, April 1, 2001.

On this day in 1992, at 4:30 PM (1630, military time), I "officially" retired. I remember being asked, that day, what I would do the next morning. I replied that I intended to set my alarm as usual that night, and then when it went off at 6 AM, I would turn it off, say "April Fool," and go back to sleep. Well I didn't need the alarm, and I couldn't go back to sleep, but I did announce "April Fool." Having worked more-or-less continuously since 1947, it was the least I could do.

And though my life has changed many times, and in many ways over those 45 years, I think the greatest changes have been in these last nine. The most significant, of course, is that we have lived in our new community since the 15th of April of that year. What changes we have made, what differences in our lives and the lives of our closest! In just dogs alone we have seen two leave us and learned to love three more. As a family we've lived through some terrible times, and some wonderful ones. We've both become different people, with new interests, new directions, new skills. We have a whole constellation of new friends and near-family; we have lost others both in and out of the family; we have found a true place of real life values and experiences.

In some ways we have discovered new facets of ourselves, and developed into new and perhaps better, but at least (one hopes) more interesting people. Tastes have changed, needs have changed, abilities have changed. Some of these are natural with aging, some are environmental, and others are just because the opportunity to try new things has presented itself when we have had the independence and the time to accept.

I suppose, for me, the greatest change has been in expanding my horizon beyond a professional vista. Yes, I have continued to pursue the same creative goals I've always sought, but I've also added a whole world of new experiences and direction. Have they changed me? Am I not basically the same person, only with a wider field of view and depth of focus? Or have I really become a different person? I think perhaps it is that I have uncovered some parts of myself that were always there, but until now I have not had the liberating opportunity to make such an extensive journey of self discovery.

And what of my life partner? Has she made this journey, too? In our long life together one of the things that has made it such a rewarding trip is that when we met we had arrived at the same station at the same time, and we have continued to travel together ever since. I have watched with joy as her horizons have expanded, too, and she has taken the opportunity to develop the parts that never had reason or opportunity to surface. What good fortune for two people to grow independently, yet together.

Am I the man I used to be, is she the woman she was, are we the couple we've always been—but never knew? We are, even as we change, getting older. Life continues to direct us, regardless of how much control we think we have.

Which leads me to a new question. If I knew what I was doing, would this be it?

Part VI—
Observation Car

About Doubt

I've heard it said that the difference between man and other animals is that man has opposable thumbs. But so do monkeys.

I've heard it said that the difference between man and animals is that man walks up-right. But so do great apes.

I've heard it said that the difference between man and lesser creatures is that man can speak. But that makes every person who cannot speak less than human.

I've heard it said that the difference between man and animals is that only man is capable of feeling. But those who believe that must never have been greeted at the end of the day by a dog.

I have heard it said that the difference between man and animals is man's ability to make and use tools. But where then do you classify birds who build nests, beavers who build dams, otters who use rocks to open mussels, and even bees who build hives? (Note I have used "who" rather than "that.")

I've heard it said that the real difference between man and animals is that only man can think something through from beginning to end, and while that may be heading in the right direction, it precludes all of those animals who hunt, who track, who kill and return with the kill to feed their families.

No, I don't think any of those attributes are unique to man. There is, in my mind, only one quality unique enough to define man as a creature apart, and alone qualified to exercise control over other animals. That is the capacity for doubt.

Other animals make choices based on instinct and learning. Man alone will approach an idea, an opportunity, an event, and expose it to doubt.

It is doubt, I believe, that leads to examination, exploration and discovery.

It is doubt that leads man to think he has a purpose in life beyond being born, living and dying.

It is doubt that brings man to a crossroads, where he may choose God, or not.

It is doubt, I believe, that allowed man to be introduced to God at all.

For without doubt, there can be no belief. There can be no trust, and finally, no faith.

Doubt, you see, leads us to try to find an answer. Doubt makes us question ourselves, others, even God. And finally, when we can answer no further, when we can discern no more, when we can no longer be satisfied with doubt, we must find faith.

Do you believe that the world was created in six days? Or do you believe that it all began with a piece of cosmic dust, and the dust swirled around and evolved into our solar system and from that, eventually, to life and man? Both ideas, it seems to me, originated in doubt: I am here today, but why? And how? To what purpose and what end? Because whether you accept the most scientific and complex theory of evolution, or the most biblical version of creation, you must believe that it all began somewhere. Where? No doubt that is something you must eventually accept on faith.

History On Ice

Yesterday we cleaned the refrigerator and its freezer. It was an enriching experience. Things buried for months found light and life for the first time in weeks. We uncovered "one-ofs"—things of which only one was left: one slice of rye bread, one half of an English muffin, a meatball, a piece of cake; in short, the kinds of things you hate to throw away, don't feel like eating, and so put back "until later."

Maybe everything is a metaphor for life, but freezers and refrigerators seem to me to store so many really good ideas put on hold. Something like the way we use our brains. So many good ideas, potential acts or actions we may do someday, get wrapped in a kind of plastic bag and put back in the freezer "for later." Only later never comes.

What about all the times you were going to call a friend and find out what was going on? Or write a letter to your congressman and tell him (or her) not only how you felt about an issue, but that you really liked what they were doing (or not doing). There are so many things we promise ourselves we are going to do, for ourselves, for others, and yet we seem so easily put off, finding it easier to wrap the ideas and put them in the refrigerator and, ultimately, in the freezer, until, like a piece of chicken, they develop unhealthy looking colors and overwhelming smells. A dead idea, I think, is just as wasted as that piece of chicken.

So we clean out the freezer and the refrigerator. We clean out drawers and closets, kitchen cabinets and attics, basements and garages. We find things we could have used, should have used, forgot about and got more of. And we put them away until we need them. It is a never ending process.

This Spring, we say, we will really clean house. Get into all of those things we've put away, stored against future need, piled up in boxes and in corners. In my office I have computer disks that no longer hold any information I want, and in fact can't run on my current hardware. There are copies of documents long since outdated, notes I can't comprehend, pencils too short to use. In the garage are parts to cars that long ago became recycled parts for other cars. There are gears and shafts and nuts and bolts that have no value, even sentimental (well, the cam shaft from my first sports car, and the grill from another are still too meaningful to throw away), but there they are. In my workshop, under the bench, are empty tool boxes, burned out electric motors, bits of wire and pieces of wood. "String too short to save."

But what about in the freezer of the mind? There I find things I put away, meaning to use, hoping to derive nourishment from, wishing to incorporate in some long-forgotten recipe. There is no way of course, to completely cleanse the freezer of the mind, except by conversion. You take what you find, wrap it in something else that is perhaps only in the refrigerator, combine it with what is in front of you on the chopping block, and cook it. Out comes some new kind of expression or perhaps a decorated cake. The ingredients are still with you, but no longer turning hard and green in some compartment of lost thoughts.

What have you stored and forgotten? Will you just keep moving the things around to make room for more? Are you saving them for later? What about telling someone you love them, need their companionship, their ideas? Can you really put that off, store it in a freezer? It is not a good idea.

Later never arrives for some things until it is too late.

Knowing You Have Wings

I was standing watching the birds the other afternoon, as they flew up to the feeders, then swooped back to the ground, or hopped from branch to branch, and I became aware of a curious thing. In particular I was watching a blue jay, as he came along a branch from the trunk of one of the pines that guard the deck. So boldly did he step that it caught my eye. This large bird, with an insouciance befitting Fred Astaire, moved easily along the branch, head up, eyes looking anywhere but down, and with nary a misstep, reached the limit of the branch, determined, I suppose, by his sense of how much the branch would support, he being a heavy bird.

And the thought occurred to me that what I was seeing was confidence. That feeling of supreme power over your environment that gives a princess royal bearing, or a general the commanding presence at the head of his troops.

It is a confidence that is part learned, part inherited, part bravado, especially on the way to becoming a general. I don't know about becoming an adult bird, but I would think it would be the same.

It's in the wings. When you know that no matter what you do in the air, you have wings to keep you aloft, that you can step off a branch in mid stride and need only spread your built-in parts and you are safe, it must have a commanding place in your mind. Perhaps parachutists develop that feeling, and pilots and even flagpole painters; something you have that will keep you safe, no matter what missteps you might take, what stumbles are in your way.

It is a state of mind, to be sure. There is something about taking your own measure of yourself, something that makes you feel sort of puffed up, I think. It squares your shoulders, puts your head up, and fearlessly commands you to step out on the limb, jump off the edge, haul yourself up and over the hurdles. It is probably what an athlete feels when the ball is in his possession, and he knows, without looking, that he is being guarded by his teammates, that he can move and the game will move with him, not the other way around. Or a surgeon when he makes the first incision.

Not hubris, not conceit. Wings.

Diversity

I think we have allowed those peculiar forces at work in our society to redefine yet another word (as with "gay" and "man" and other simple concepts). We hear the word used so often by those who would change our world, that we begin to accept diversity as they have defined it: non-Caucasian, female, two-mommy or two-daddy families. In fact, diversity is a real word, with real meaning, and one we cannot let go of so easily.

We are diverse because we are people. What is good for the modern city dweller in the occidental world just doesn't have meaning to a peasant in the Orient. What works in a city of a quarter of a million people falls flat when you try to apply it 50 miles away in a rural community of a few hundred.

And striving for diversity is truly a good thing. By encouraging it we stimulate growth in ourselves as human beings. We find new answers to old problems, even uncover causes we never suspected, or concerns we might never have had.

Still, we grow, and through growth we may become what evolution has been striving all these years to achieve: one species with every possible combination and permutation that in the end (and the end will come) will explain why it all began in the first place.

Even if we never do, in this lifetime, learn why it all began, or even how, we might—just might—begin to glimpse the pattern of it, the structure and form we must follow to whatever purpose there is. For you see, when we begin to think that all of this life is constructed for our own purposes, we lose sight of the reality: life, in its every form and kind, is all part of a single, forward thrusting motion.

Preacher

My friend is a preacher. Not a minister, not a reverend. A preacher. He tells me where he stands, what he believes, what is right and wrong. No shilly-shally, no maybe, no "situation." Right is right and wrong is wrong.

We may disagree on theology; we certainly are not of the same mind with regard to denomination. But right is right and wrong is wrong, and we agree on that.

My friend is a preacher, a rock in a world of sand sculptures. He knows what he believes, and he believes what he knows.

We spend far too little of our time together along the banks of rivers and lakes, fishing ostensibly for scaled creatures. Often, though, our time is really about ideas, testing observations and revelations about ourselves, about our fellow men and women, about children and the world we are preparing for them. Our discussions are never confrontational. It would do no good. My friend believes what he believes. He is as strong as a locust and as tough as an oak when it comes to what he knows is right and wrong. Yet he will consider any point of view, any new insight into what I believe, and he will even discuss it. Calmly, searchingly, but without bombast and thunder. A rock doesn't need to thunder.

Sometimes we talk about a specific problem. One that might confront me, or one he might be wrestling with. You see, even the strongest, most immovable rock can be battered by wind and sand and rain. That doesn't mean it necessarily will roll over, but even a rock can have the ground cut out from under it. So it pays to be aware of change and shift. But still remain a rock.

Most of the time, when we aren't engaged in some discussion of the size or breed of a fish, we will talk about his congregation, and explore specific problems he must deal with. Or it might be a wall I face and must climb. Either way, we dig into, probe, examine our own beliefs, to assure ourselves, I guess, that they are still true. I have my own way of seeing, and often the things I see are not clear. I need my friend the preacher to help me clear away what obscures, assist me in my own quest for the right path ahead of me. That is what a preacher does.

Yes, he ministers, too. He consoles and uplifts those in dark despair. He prays, for he believes in that with all his heart, and he sometimes convinces me that I need to do that too. It isn't something I have done a lot of, but when he helps me I find it natural and inspiring and comforting. Occasionally I go to his church of a Sunday (though I'm a Jew, not a Christian), because he preaches, and his preaching always gives me something. No matter the kind of day, when he begins to preach his face reflects a light not falling anywhere else in the sanctuary. He truly glows with fulfillment when he sermonizes. And what he preaches is good to hear, to think about, to probe in my own mind in the days that follow. Sometimes I will write him a response, or go to his study and, if we can't go on to the river, spend some time in discussion of his sermon. Once in a while, he tells me, I present him with some thoughts that lead him to another sermon, so on balance, we push each other.

I'm not nearly the rock he is, for though I am a little older, my beliefs are, in some ways, less firm than his. Perhaps I have seen more, questioned more than he. Perhaps it is just that I am not as round a rock: more a somewhat rougher, irregularly shaped stone. I still have very ambivalent beliefs. I do believe that above all, there must be some grand scheme—God or Nature—into which this all fits. I somehow can't make the leap so many have, to believe in a power that will be there after "life," but neither can I totally refute it. I have to wonder, if God is watching, what kind of sense of humor He has, to let humans behave toward each other as they do; to have created so many visions of His plan. Still, I don't know what else there is— maybe nothing. I know that everything is linked: virtue and evil, day and night, strength and weakness, hate and love.

    My friend is a preacher. He has the answers. All you have to do is listen. It is the sound of a rock standing firm.

About Trust

A local youth program began its fourth season recently, and I attended the kick-off picnic at the Presbyterian church. Most of my family has been involved in the program since its inception, and I have enjoyed watching the community investment and involvement grow.

During the first two years I worked with the young people in a project to cut and put together bird houses. My youngest granddaughter, Elisabeth, and I had worked out a simple, easily assembled box, and over several weeks I provided instruction and assistance as youngsters from six to fifteen cut, drilled and nailed the boxes together.

It was exciting for me to see little hands master some basic carpentry skills, and learn to take pride in doing something that was truly a "hands on" experience. Sometimes the builders would work individually, but as the project went along I was able to turn more and more of the work over to teams that competed to see who could build the most bird houses in a single session. It was easy to see who was a natural leader, who wanted to learn, who had good work habits, and who could be directed in developing new skills.

At the end of the first year we had built enough bird houses so that each member of the group could take one home. The second year we had a surplus that went to market during the annual Maple Festival, and actually earned some income for the program. From his saw mill at Doe Hill, a local sawyer supplied beautiful pine boards each Fall, and except for buying nails and drill bits, we had no other expenses. Arch received one of the first houses, signed by all of those who participated in the project.

One of the lasting effects of the birdhouse program has been the bond established among all of us who worked on the project. In the manner of Highland County we wave, we call out "hello," and though they have changed and grown each year, I know a lot of the future of our county by name and nature.

The program not only brings children together with each other, but with adults of the community who volunteer their time to teach, to direct games, to prepare the evening meal, and to serve as table parents during dinner. With guidance and love, each helps the other, and all benefit.

It is so often the way here. The medical center, the fire departments, the rescue squad, as well as some of the service organizations, have junior members who volunteer and really throw themselves into the community service projects that are part of the Highland County way. It is through that kind of interaction, I think, that we pass on the sense of community responsibility and caring for others that makes our county unique in the "me first" age.

I began thinking about what a program like this can mean to the young people of our community, and what they will carry with them into adulthood. That led to thoughts again about those two years of birdhouse building. I knew what the children had learned: teamwork, some manual skills, some respect for wood and for the tools they used, and the satisfying feeling that comes from taking parts and putting them together in a practical and useful way. Working with my hands, especially with wood, has always seemed to me an apt metaphor for the way in which one may craft a life from the materials at hand. I believe that the earlier one learns that he can convert a simple piece of raw material into a useful and attractive object, the more likely that person is to remain in control of his life later on. But what had I gotten from that process? Let me put it this way: if you can hold a three-penny finishing nail, while a six-year-old swings her hammer down, you both have defined forever the real meaning of trust.

About The Meandering Path of Coincidence

I had my monthly flat tire this afternoon. That in itself isn't unusual. In fact I believe I can say without being accused of embellishment that since I have lived in Highland County I have had more flat tires than in all previous years combined.

When I was in college I drove cars I bought for $25 or $50, so you can imagine the kind of tires I used then. Of course in the 50's new tires were usually around $20, and a quart of oil was a quarter (what was known as "reprocessed"—the kind that came in a glass bottle with a galvanized metal spout). Gasoline was less than fifteen cents a gallon, too.

Anyway, you could buy a recapped tire for about half the cost of a new one, and tires seemed to last a long time. Of course in a $25 car I probably didn't drive as fast as most rush-hour traffic does today; still I did get around. I put eight—or ten-thousand miles a year on a car, just cruisin'.

I don't really remember having flat tires, except on long trips. I remember driving from New York City to Greensboro, North Carolina in 1954. I had a '40 Hudson and somewhere around Edison, on the recently completed New Jersey Turnpike, the old horse threw a shoe. I managed to crunch off at an exit ramp to a local garage, where for about five dollars I bought a used tire, had it mounted and was on my way again.

What with the condition of the other tires, the age of the vehicle, and the summer heat, the 550-mile trip took about 24 hours. Flat tires and overheating were commonplace then, when people drove cars that old and older as a matter of course. The Hudson had belonged to an uncle who turned it over to me after he was finished with it, and I was bringing it to North Carolina for the summer. At the time, as I recall, he had a '46 Ford wood-bodied convertible, a '52 Buick, and a '39 Pontiac. In those years that wasn't a collection, as it would be today, but rather just what you had around to get you where you were going. He was also the only one in his household who drove, so he didn't really miss the Hudson when I drove it away.

I'm sure I had other flat tires in other cars, and in other places, but they were neither memorable, nor frequent. Here, living on a gravel road, having a gravel driveway, tires seem to be much more vulnerable than they used to be. One tire I replaced a month ago had six plugs in it by the time the tread was worn down to the limit. At one point it even occurred to me to go and look at the road to see how state department of transportation managed to get all of the stones to bed point up. I thought that maybe they had a new machine that did it, but I decided that it was just coincidence: my tires coincided with the edge of the stone.

So after all of this, what makes today's flat remarkable enough to write about? Well, I was at the local medical center talking with the executive director and about ready to leave, when her daughter showed up on her way to work. It was raining and I was about to leave, so I offered to drive her to the restaurant where she worked. As I started out of that parking lot I saw another friend and I stopped to chat. While we were talking, the restaurant's owner came over to the car and said, "You've got a tire going flat. We've been standing inside watching it go down!" (And people wonder what we do for entertainment in the country!) I got out and looked, and sure enough, the tire was about down to the rim. I said a hasty "thanks and goodbye" and drove (slowly) across the street to the gas station where, in a few minutes the tire was repaired, the car again sitting level and square.

On the way home I began thinking about the sequence of events that had me in the car going home (in the rain), without having to pull over and change the tire myself. If I hadn't offered to take Jessica to the pizza place—well, if I hadn't committed myself to bring something to the rescue squad building—as a matter of fact if I hadn't stopped by the medical center—anyway, you see the pattern. One thing leads to another, and sometimes things work out as if you had planned them, when all along it was just coincidence.

And then I remembered something I had read a while back, written by an unknown author: "Coincidence is God's way of remaining anonymous."

Which may even explain who "Anonymous" might be.

Just "Now"

I think heaven must be hell for those who are at least Type "A" personalities. For those of us who are worse—the self-starters, the insomniacs, the congenitally hyperactive over-scheduled pushers, movers, shakers—what could be worse than to be in a place where not only do you have nothing to do, you can't even communicate it to the ones you left behind! Can you imagine sitting on some marble bench in a cloud of trees watching those you know plod on doing things without your direction? Without your motivation?

I'm a year away from 75, and I still can't enjoy doing nothing! I tried fishing, but that was worse than golf, or running or even becoming a wine connoisseur. I mean, how many times can you get a headache before you realize that something so intensely personal as playing a game or drinking wine is not for you?

Heaven, for me, is being exactly where I am, but without obligations. I still can't go into my shop and fool around with pieces of wood left over from some major job around the farm, or go down to the barn and work on my 60 year old tractor, or just enjoy riding around the fields mowing hay I don't need without thinking about all the things I "should" be doing. I don't even walk in the woods with the dogs without a roll of red surveyor's tape in my pocket in case I see a tree that can be taken down and cut up for fire wood.

Over the years I've had ideas for inventions I'd like to make, and tools I could learn to master, or jobs I'd like to do just to see if I could do them. But when I set myself a time to work on something like that, I feel guilty, knowing there are so many other things that I should do: clean gutters, rake rocks in the driveway, stain the deck, just the kinds of things we need to do to maintain a "maintenance-free" home.

Part of the problem, I think, is that I'm aware of the many things that need doing, and I'm afraid that if I stop to do things just because I want to, I'll have things undone when I can't do them any longer. Is that a penalty of growing older? Perhaps it is a justified concern, and I'm rushing to "get everything done" in time. In time for what? No matter how many times I clean the gutters, or cut the grass the leaves still fall, and the grass continues to grow (thankfully). Is hell a place were the grass doesn't grow and the leaves don't fall? I cannot imagine a universe in which things don't change and where nothing repeats itself.

I keep looking for the way that lets me shed responsibility and concern for tomorrow. I know I should be savoring every day (I really think I do) by enjoying what is immediately before me, and not focusing on tomorrow, but somehow there never seems time to simply sit and contemplate things—to "think a little think," as Pooh said. (Was it Pooh? Was it Eyore? I haven't time to go look it up.) I'd really like to believe in my own mantra: "Another damned beautiful Highland County day: too nice to work."

If the end is the beginning, where is the now?

Part VII—Mixed Freight

Making a Mark

I was sitting in a rocking chair on the front porch of the local historical society museum the other day, enjoying the unusually warm November day. It was a quiet time, when the afternoon visitors hadn't yet found their way to the building, leaving me, as the "docent-in-charge" with little to do. Always a creative time.

It was a breezy afternoon, and the "open" flags were whipping about, alternately spelling "OPN" and "PEN" and, occasionally, "NEPO" with the letters reversed. Given the setting, and my own interest in words, it was perhaps natural that my mind would begin to speculate on the origins of writing, and the names of letters.

Looking at the "N" on the flag made me wonder, first of all, why we call it an "en" rather than something more descriptive, like "halfanem" or, conversely, why "em" is not called "doubleen." After all, we have "double you" for the letter that actually looks like a double vee unless you write in rounded letters; an affectation I always thought was limited to the girls I knew in high school.

Anyway, after I put those thoughts aside, I began to think about the first person to make a mark on a cave wall or a piece of skin, and give it a name. Sitting around the campfire of an evening, I imagine this guy in his rustic garb thinking to himself, "Now if I can get Og to understand that this is the first letter of his name, maybe we can leave messages for each other about where the mastodon has gone."

I wondered, too, what the first written word might have been. It could have been a name, certainly it was a name for something, otherwise why would you want a word in the first place? Pointing, waving, grunting would all be useful ways of communicating most things, of course. And there were already words in use, I'm certain. So what would make an otherwise busy man take up a piece of charcoal from the fire and start scribbling? Could it have been the first instance of "Kilroy was here?" Or was it, as I suggested earlier, more important than that: "Follow me to the mastodon."

Whatever the reason, I knew I owed a huge debt to the man who invented writing. Then I thought, "Was it a man?" And the answer almost certainly had to be "Yes." A man, you see, would be the one who had time to devote to such obscure pursuits. His mate would have been too busy to find the time for such nonsense. There was no reason to write "Do the laundry," or "Pick up skins from floor," or even "Roast tiger for dinner." The person who conceived the "you know what I'm talking about" conversational gambit had no time to waste on words, anyway. Of course it was natural for her to embrace the technology once her man demonstrated it to her. Maybe the first note was "Og, the mastodon went west." But I'll bet the second one was "1lb onon, 1 frsh pterodactyl brst, 2 yams, bnch grapes."

Man could really appreciate that!

Free Speech

Adversity can strengthen or destroy a person. Learning to defend oneself, and a culture that permits it, strengthens not only the individual, but the community as well. As a Jew growing up in the South in the 30's and 40's it was often difficult to know how to counter taunts and comments from other children and some adults that amounted to, by today's definition, "hate speech." The only thing that made it possible was that while the Constitution allows freedom of speech, it also forbids, through the prohibition of state religion, any government support of such speech. Unlike other countries, where anti-Semitism was often a matter of public policy, and therefore subtly if not blatantly encouraged, America relied on the freedom the Jewish community has always felt to express and defend itself against words or acts. Today we, like other religious, racial and social groups thrive and prosper (and often get along quite well), despite egregious displays and proposals (even by politicians) that would use differences to separate and divide for personal gain. Take away the freedom to express ourselves and we take away America's most unique and important part of the social contract: the freedom to reply, correct and even chastise critics and self-appointed destroyers of America.

A Christmas Story

I live in a very small community, a county of only 2,400 people, and only 6 of us are Jews. The rest are Baptists and Methodists and Presbyterians and Lutherans and Brethren and Mennonite and Episcopalian and Evangelicals and Adventists and probably a few others. So we are not exactly a "presence" here in the mountains along Virginia's Northwest frontier. But we are all active in the community, and some of us are perhaps more visible than others. Most of us are married to Christians, and so we celebrate each other's holidays and holy days, and sometimes attend each other's services. The nearest synagogue, and the one I belong to, is anywhere from a 70 mile to a 120 mile round-trip, depending on where we live in the county.

So it was, on Christmas night, 2004, that I found myself saying a hurried goodbye to our daughter and granddaughters, and my wife, as I left the house to respond to what the 9-1-1 dispatcher reported as a "female who has fallen, possible broken leg." It took me ten minutes to reach the ambulance two mountains away, and another ten for my driver to get us to the house where the accident occurred. As we pulled up in front of the gate leading to the double-wide, set back along a muddy track away from the gravel road, a few neighbors approached the truck. One, a little "happier" than the others, assured us that we were not needed, a fact confirmed by the husband who came out from the trailer home to meet us. His wife, he said, had simply fallen, but hadn't broken her leg. I got out of the truck and took my bag, saying that as long as we were here, I would just make sure she was ok. Sometimes that can spark a protest, but this time the husband accompanied me down the track to the cinder block steps without objection. After opening the door, and showing me where his wife was, he disappeared into another room.

On the sofa I found the heavy-set wife, her equally round daughter, and a miniature version of them both, the granddaughter. The patient was sitting up, with her legs across the granddaughter's lap. The young girl, probably 12 or 13, was applying ice to the injured knee, and the child's mother was just sitting, looking worried.

After reassuring myself that there was no broken bone, not even a cut, and discussing the options with the patient, and giving the granddaughter more specific instructions about the application of the ice pack, I began writing my report. The granddaughter took advantage of a break in the talk to ask, "Do you go to church?" I replied that I did, and she asked me where. "I belong to a temple in Staunton," I replied. "What faith is that?" she asked. "I'm Jewish," I replied. "You're Jewish?" she asked. "Aren't the Jewish people God's chosen people? I wish I was Jewish," she said. "Then I'd be one of the chosen people." "I think we are all God's chosen people," I responded. At that point, her brother, whom I had not noticed standing opposite the sofa, said, "I wish I was Jewish." There was a pause, then the nine-year old continued: "Then I'd get presents for eight days!"

I wished them all a Merry Christmas, and stepped outside, grateful for the fresh air and black, star-filled sky, and my life in a community where such conversations are conducted with love.

About Bugs

The coming millennium was much on my mind in 1999, as this essay demonstrates.

The subject is "bugs." Now, the word is one which has come to mean anything from insects in general to almost anything unexplained and annoying. Bugs at a picnic, bugs in a plan, even bugs in the brain.

It seems to me that bugs of any sort are not just something to be overcome. They are part of God's plan and purpose; each has a place, however distasteful to humans, in the grand scheme. We have already seen the consequences of man's attempts to eradicate bugs: they just grow stronger and more persistent, or they disappear, creating a hole through which vital forces spill and disappear. Only man sees himself as more necessary than insects or "bugs."

Even man-made bugs appear because we have made a place for them. Y2K isn't there because a malevolent computer created it; it exists because of the shortsightedness of early computer engineers and software designers. Y2K is an early warning that those same characteristics may have been put into (or left out of) other designs that could have far greater consequences than an incorrect date calculator.

HAL, in *2001—A Space Odyssey*, is one of the best known fictional voices to call attention to over-reliance on "artificial intelligence," but science fiction writers have been sounding the alarm since the earliest days of that genre. The hand of man is not the hand of God directly applied, but one that is filtered through each individual's experiences, biases and desires.

Manners

We live in a place we like to think of as under-crowded. There are about 2300 people who live in the county, and that makes it a very small place, indeed. But then again, it isn't a very large area, either: about 470 square miles. We've been places were there are more people, but the space is so vast that you hardly notice them.

Away out west, where the spaces are marked by fences too far away to see, and so much of it looks the same anyway, I have noticed something kind of rare these days: good manners. Not that the folks hereabouts aren't friendly and caring and all of that New Age stuff, but still, there are times...

One of the things I noticed out west was that with all of those rocks in the Colorado desert, and in the Rocky Mountains, in the Grand Tetons and Yellowstone, there is no graffiti! Nobody (at least since the westward migration ended), seems to have gotten out a spray can and put names and symbols and cute sayings anywhere that I could see. Of course, it might just be that the rocks are too hard to get to (except we drove through canyons where the rocks were right beside the road), or too forbidding (snow in July, for goodness sake), but I noted some other things out west, as well.

One Sunday afternoon, in Cody, Wyoming, we decided to go to a movie. Of course the building only had four theaters, but otherwise it was just like any other place these days—except for one thing: before the movie started, before the previews, there was no cutesy little film telling you to turn off your cell phones, deposit your trash in the trash bins, and most startling of all, no admonition to BE QUIET! Frankly, I was a little nervous before the feature began, because I'm one of those people who get really upset when others talk during a movie. I think it is most unmannerly, and it often ruins a film for me, if I have to be constantly asking strangers to stop talking. I shouldn't have to, but....

Anyway, the movie played, and not once was there an interruption form the audience: no phone beeping, no "Now she's gonna..." from some uncouth yokel behind me, and no trash on the floors! Now maybe this was a once-in-a-lifetime audience, but I didn't get that impression. Anyway, we made our way out of the theater, got in the car and headed off to Bubba's BarBeQue for dinner, thinking all the while how pleasant it had been in the theater.

In the restaurant (where we had to wait about 20 minutes for a table (worth it), we felt very comfortable with the wait, and the large group of people (about 20) waiting with us. All very pleasant and mannerly. It made me think of the wide open spaces out there, and consider that perhaps it is the lack of crowded places, the distance between not just places, but people, when you live with neither human nor visual crowding. Here where we are, the mountains surround and enfold us. I like that. But out there, you are really on your own, really in the best possible kind of place for relaxing and feeling away from it all. Especially away from the pressure of too many people.

Hey, Joe!

This short piece was prompted by a news report sometime in the 1990s, about athletes selling their autographs.

I'm not much of a baseball fan, nor in fact am I a fan of any sport, but when Joe DiMaggio died, I was immediately reminded of when I was a kid, and DiMaggio was still playing ball. I remembered that there had been a time when I knew who played what, and even went to ball games.

Somewhere between high school and entering the real world of work I lost touch with that part of my life, and more or less put it out of my mind. In the intervening years I have not seen a "real" game beyond 5th or 6th grade soccer, and I just can't sit still long enough to watch a game on tv. In fact I have never enjoyed being just a viewer. Somehow, being in the ball park makes you a participant. Sitting at home is such a passive way to participate in anything.

What really came into my mind as I read the obituaries about Joe DiMaggio was that his death says more about the death of heroes than about him. He was, by all accounts, an intensely private man, who knew his own worth, but held that to himself, more than most.

When I read today of sports figures who charge for their autographs I think that says it all: these men have sold themselves, and have only their name left to market. Yes they are celebrities, and yes they can command extortionate salaries for playing kids' games, but they are not models for young people to follow, unless they want to achieve a kind of negative image.

Granite in Sandstone

"The puritan ethic," that awful and menacing phrase describing the backbone in those of us of a certain age, is rather like a streak of granite running through a sandstone layer. It signifies a certain kind of approach to life and living. Pleasure is not, according to this doctrine, something you pursue. Instead, it is something that comes to you in the pursuit of other things.

We were discussing the concept of the puritan ethic as a forcing field or cold frame for the development of a personal style of living. In young people it seems to be missing and is replaced instead by a demand for "happiness" all the time. What so many young people seem to miss is that happiness, being happy, is a transitory, passing moment, not an eternal way of life. The only time it may possibly become eternal is when one achieves the "eternal life" so highly promoted by most religions.

Written in the Stars

We spent a quiet evening looking at the sky the other night. It was different from other views, in that we did it through a telescope in an observatory on a dark hill. It is an amateur astronomy club's telescope, and so isn't exactly a Hubble image, but it was enough to help us achieve closer encounters with the stars.

The group attending ranged from junior teens to senior middle-agers, only one of whom had ever experienced looking at the sky through a roll back roof that wasn't on a car. It was a different view.

Listening to the astronomer-in-chief, an advanced amateur who admits to nearly 50 years of such nocturnal habit, I was struck not by the immensity of the known universe—the number of stars, suns, galaxies—as much as by the unfathomable size of what we don't know, can't see, do not know how to interpret.

For years I have tried to come to grips with what I call the "C" factor: the earth is but one planet among many, in one solar system among many, in one galaxy among many, and they all started from some sort of cosmic incident or accident. Before that there was darkness and void. But even darkness and void are descriptions of something, even if it is negative space. So before that, there was "C."

If we are to disappear in four million years or so, if our system is to be inhaled into a black hole, if truly it is a matter of "dust to dust," then Einstein was right, and all matter is permanent but not rigid; it can change form but be neither created nor destroyed. So we must go to something, somewhere, in some form.

The questions raised are not new questions, of that I am supremely aware. Still, it is the unanswered question that should and must remain unanswered until we have crossed from this life into what ever lies beyond—if there is a beyond.

As the astronomer said: "If there is such a thing as a Black Hole, and all the matter is drawn into it, does it come out the other side?" Is there another side?

It makes you reevaluate your own telescopic view of yourself, doesn't it? You want to be sure you aren't looking at it through the wrong end.

Memory

I've noticed, in the last few years, a tendency toward what must be drop-outs in the tape of memory. There was a time when, if I put something down, I could visualize the act, and the steps preceding it, to locate whatever I had moved. Lately, though, I find that I can take a screw out of something, for instance, put it down on the work bench, do whatever I was going to do that required removing the screw, and then—and then—I can't find the screw. Well. It could have fallen to the floor, or rolled under something else, but what makes it doubly frustrating is that no matter how hard I try I can't bring up a moving picture of the steps I took to move and put down the missing screw. Does that ever happen to you?

I suppose it could be that I am simply on auto-pilot some of the time, and taking something apart, employment I have enjoyed since I was probably three years old, has become so routinized in my mind that I no longer make mental note of what I am doing. I don't think so.

It would be nice to think that my mind is so full of important stuff that small details slip past the memory guards and simply wander around in my brain. But that really isn't it, I know. It is something else. Three score have come and gone, and the ten is exhausted, so maybe it is just that there is so much accumulated "stuff" (as in a seldom visited attic) that small things, like screws and nails and paper clips (the stuff that holds stuff together) are just insignificant enough to disappear. Not when you are trying to put something back together again, however.

Then they become the (I can't remember the word) that holds everything together.

It's nice to have a mind like a steel trap. The only trouble is, unless you keep it well lubricated, it will rust.

Conversation

"You really like this old junk, don't you?" The younger man idly kicked the tire on the old truck, as if to emphasize his disdain.

"Well, yeah," I laughed. "It serves." We were standing on either side of the front of the old truck, elbows on the hood, talking about what I needed to do with the body.

Lifting his hat briefly to scratch his head, and then reposition the cap, he stared off into some future car lot. "Not me. If I had the money I'd never buy anything old," he said, giving the sentence a kind of shake as he let it out. Almost like a dog ready to discard an old bone. "I don't think I want somebody else's problems. Got enough of my own." He brushed his hand over the dusty paint. "'sides, man with your money shouldn't be gettin' his hands dirty with all this old grease."

I smiled, thinking how many people seem to believe that when you are older you are either financially secure or ready for the poor house. "Even if I could afford it," I said, "I really do get a kick out of getting something running that other people would just throw away."

This truck, recently picked up from a young man who had given up on getting it on the road, was a good example. It was nearly 20 years old, but I had taken it on to replace one that was over thirty, and had truly outlived its usefulness. Yes, it had holes in the body, and lots of things didn't work as well as they could, but most were minor. A burned out light, a loose door hinge, rattles and squeaks and clunks that, until I had put a muffler on it, I hadn't even heard. But it was strong where it counted: four-wheel drive, plenty of power to push a snow blade in the winter, and the price was right. Besides, it was summer now, and I had several months to patch the holes in the cab and doors, make sure the heater worked, and in general get it ready for its main job of keeping the long driveway open in winter. Much better for me to use than the little open tractor I cleared with now. Besides, it was a farm vehicle: carrying things from one field to another, running down to the general store for fuel or over the mountain for a needed tractor part, hauling trash to the land fill a mile-and-a-half away.

Long before I came here to our now fallow farm, I had become adept at resurrecting old machinery and tools. Part of it had to do with necessity, of course, and part with a sense of loss each time something once useful had to be discarded. Over the years I had collected carpentry tools, mechanics tools and even bits and pieces of machinery that I was not always able to identify. Some I simply cleaned up and put on the shelf, or in a box. Some I made work again, others became part of something else, finding a new purpose. There is something about a tool or piece of machinery that begs (in my mind, at least) not to be discarded until the last bit of usefulness has been extracted. Sculptors talk about the stone or wood speaking to them, telling them where to cut and chip and hammer. Old tools, old machines do the same with me. I look, and hold, and listen. Then, at some point, something happens, and I understand the piece, and we work together to find utility.

"Well, I don't know," the younger man continued, pushing his thought out into the sunlight for examination. "Seems to me you're always fixing and putting off getting important jobs done, just keeping all this stuff running." We surveyed the truck, and the nearly 60 year-old tractor parked beside it in the field. We had come down to discuss whether or not the hay would be useful to him when I got it cut. "I remember last year when it took you all summer to finish this one field. Did you ever figure out what was making the tractor quit?"

"Sure," I said, "it was the ignition coil. Old guy in town tested it for me. He's been working on these tractors since they were new." The young man was right, of course. I had interrupted the cutting of the fields several times over the summer because the engine would run an hour, then stop. Run then stop. Let it sit for a while and it was ready to go again. "Well, I wasn't in any hurry then, you know." I paused to look down the field, scanning the tall grass waiting for the mower. "Not in any hurry this year, really, unless you want it. I'll cut it once, maybe twice, but if you don't want to come and bale it, I can take my time. It won't go anywhere." There are only two small fields, one of about 5 acres and the other about twenty, out of the 160 we own. We once had some sheep and chickens, but now about all we grow are rocks and trees. I guess they fit in with my feelings about keeping old things around as long as I can.

Oh, it can be frustrating, when you once make up your mind to go and do a job, then find the tool or piece of equipment needs something before you can start. Not nearly as frustrating as starting a job and having to stop to make a repair, but that is the nature of men and machines, I think. As we get older we learn to pace ourselves, or the "machinery" does it for us. Let it rest, cool down, catch its breath, and it is ready to go again. Not a bad formula for a man, either. A kind of natural principle of energy conservation.

The young man repositioned his hat again, eyed the hay, said, "Well, guess I'll come bale it when you're ready. Old trucks and tractors might be ok, but old hay won't be a help to anybody." His hat now resettled, he gave the old hood a bump with his fist, and got back in his own shiny year-old pickup. "Call me when it's down—the hay, not the tractor." He laughed, and drove away.

Why the Chicken Crosses the Road

Why does the chicken cross the road? I suppose for the same reason that deer, squirrels, cats, mice, frogs and snakes do.

I was pondering just this question recently, because it seems to me that all too often I dodge one animal or another as I drive along our country roads. Perhaps you have noticed it yourself; a squirrel chasing a nut is flicking himself along a roadway, near one side, when you come up on him. Just as you are about to pass, he darts across the road, appearing to be aiming directly for your wheels. You brake or twist or just close your eyes, and…there is no jolt, no bump, and in your rearview mirror, no squashed animal.

The same thing happens with all the other wild life. On our road, ruffed grouse and wild turkey, not to mention the occasional bear, use the roadway at their convenience. Well, ok, that's fine with me. I know birds like to take dust baths, and what better place than one of the highway department's "secondary" roads? And the bears, of course, have been coming this way from mountain top to river, for longer than man has chased (or run from) bruin.

What I guess I don't understand is why the smaller animals, especially, wait until you are coming along, and then dash out, from one side to the other. Is it like people in some cultures who try to escape their bad karma by dashing in front of a car, hoping the spirit will be run over? Well, the same thing happens to them that happens to the raccoon or opossum or polecat.

So why does the chicken cross the road? The answer we learned as children, "to get to the other side," somehow doesn't seem adequate, given the consequences. Now, you would think that if the answer is "because that's the way they've always done it," or "they were crossing there long before the road was built," that these genetically directed habits would, over the millennia, be modified in the course of things. I mean, if viruses can evolve the way they do (between colds), why wouldn't deer eventually be reprogrammed to stay away from roads? They do a fine job of disappearing when hunting season begins, I know that.

I really don't know the answer to the question, which is somewhat frustrating, because I spend a lot of time jinking down the road to miss the wildlife. I'd rather look at it, watch it scamper up a hillside or lope across a field, instead of worrying about hitting it. In fact, what I'd very much like to do is sit down calmly with any one of them and ask the question, "Why does the chicken cross the road?" Could it be, as with so much in our lives, that the answer is no more or less than the one we've always heard? Man tends to do things over and over, even though the consequences are clear. We are simply moving from one place in life to the next, and consequences are a part of living. Without them, we just might always end up where we were headed.

The End